How to build a website

FOR
KIDS

AGES 12 - 18

Copyright © 2021 S Basu
All rights reserved.

Disclaimer:

The information and materials presented here are for educational purposes only. Every effort has been made to make this book as complete and as accurate as possible but no warranty or fitness is implied. The information provided is on an "as is" basis. The ideas and opinions expressed are of the author's own imagination and the author is not affiliated to any organization, school or educational discipline and will not be held accountable or liable for any inadvertent misrepresentation.

Contents

CHAPTER 1: INTRODUCTION 4
    1.1 : WHAT IS HTML? 4
    1.2 : WHAT ARE HTML ATTRIBUTES? 6
    1.3 : WHAT IS CSS? 6
    1.4 : DOWNLOAD AND INSTALL NOTEPAD++ 6

CHAPTER 2: HTML 11
    2.1 : HEADINGS 15
    2.2 : PARAGRAPH 18
    2.3 : LINKS 19
    2.4 : IMAGE 22
    2.5 : TABLES 25
    2.6 : LIST 29
    2.7 : DROP DOWN MENU 32
    2.8 : INPUT TAGS 34
    2.9 : HTML FORM 36

CHAPTER 3: CSS 42
    COMMONLY USED CSS PROPERTIES 42
    3.1 : INTERNAL CSS 45
        3.1.1 : Add a background image to the web page 48
        3.1.2 : Set a height and width 50
        3.1.3 : Add a Heading 51
        3.1.4 : Add a list of link 56
        3.1.5 : Add a table 66
        3.1.6 : Add a drop down menu 72
        3.1.7 : Add input fields 78
        3.1.8 : Add an image 83
    3.2 : EXTERNAL CSS 87
    3.3 : IN-LINE CSS 95

CHAPTER 4 : ASSESSMENT 97

Chapter 1: Introduction

In order to build a website, you need to have a strong understanding of HTML and CSS.

1.1 : What is HTML?

- HTML stands for Hyper Text Markup Language.

- HTML elements help to design a web page and they are represented with open and close tags. Example: (open tag) < *element_name* > ...... </ *element_name* > (close tag)

HTML document is divided into **head** and the **body**.

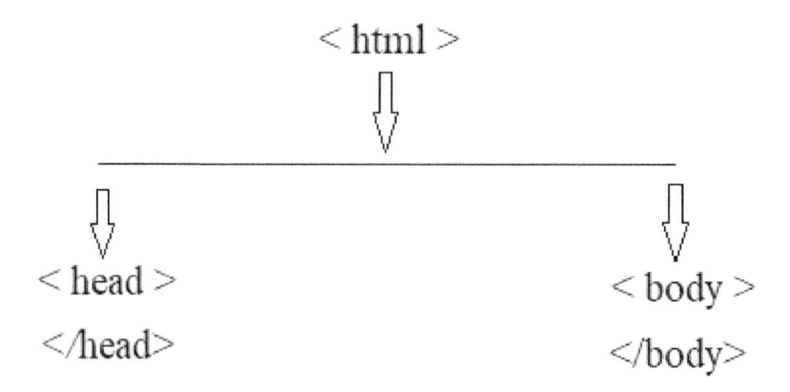

```
            < html >
               ⇓
    _____
       ⇓                    ⇓
    < head >             < body >
    </head>              </body>
```

- The **<head>** contains all information about a web page. Example: CSS etc

- The <body> contains the main content of the web page which will get displayed to the user.

Example:

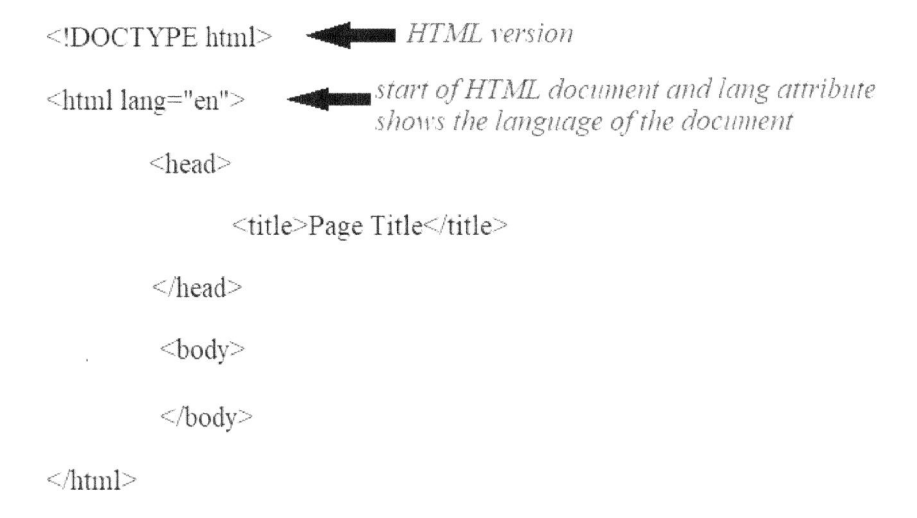

```
<!DOCTYPE html>         ⬅ HTML version
<html lang="en">        ⬅ start of HTML document and lang attribute
                           shows the language of the document
    <head>
        <title>Page Title</title>
    </head>
    <body>
    </body>
</html>
```

Important points to note from the above piece of code are:

1. **DOCTYPE** stands for **Document type** and the line **<!DOCTYPE html>** denotes the HTML version. This line of code must be written in the beginning of all HTML documents.

2. All HTML codes must be written within **<html>** tags.

3. The **<head>** tag contains title of the web page within **<title>** tags.

4. The **<body>** tag contains the main content of the web page which will get displayed to the user.

5

1.2 : What are HTML attributes?

HTML attributes provides some additional information about a HTML element.
(We will learn about few very important HTML attributes as we proceed further).

1.3 : What is CSS?

CSS stands for Cascading Style Sheets and is mainly used to make a HTML document pretty and presentable.

Before we start coding, we need a text editor to write our code and for that we will be using **Notepad++.**

1.4 : Download and Install Notepad++

- Open Google Chrome browser *(or any browser you like)*, search for **<u>download notepad++</u>** and click on the website highlighted in the screen shot below.

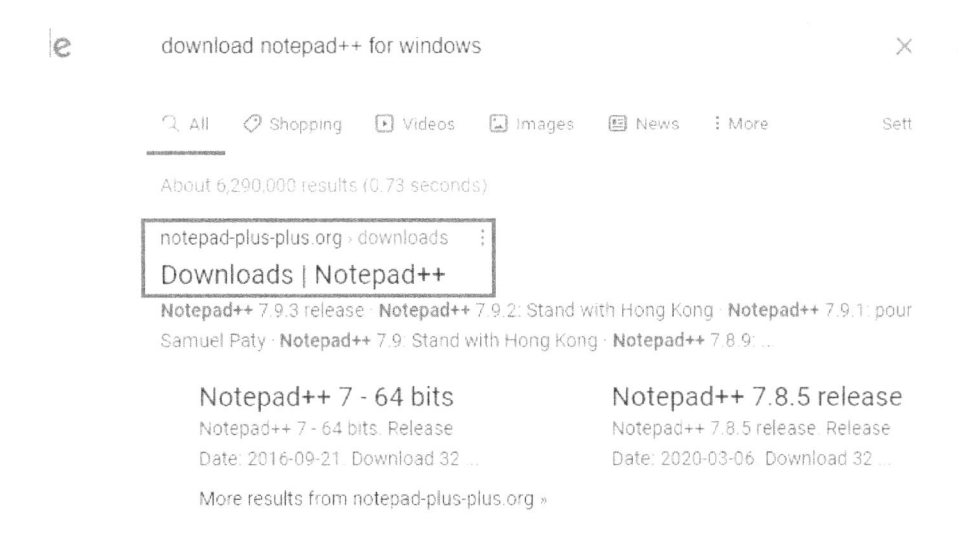

- Select the latest **Notepad**++ version for download

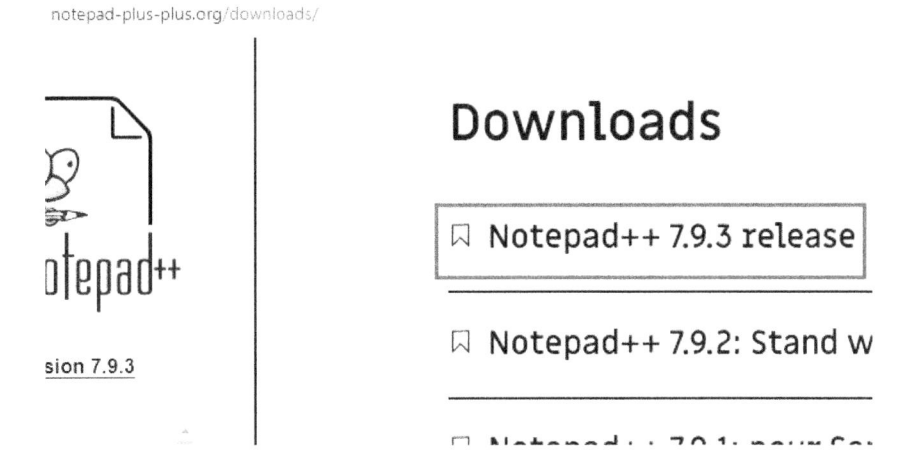

- Scroll down and download the 64-bit Installer for windows.

Download 64-bit x64

Installer | GPG Signature
- Portable (zip) | GPG Signature
- Portable (7z) | GPG Signature
- Mini-portable (7z) | GPG Signatu

Download source code

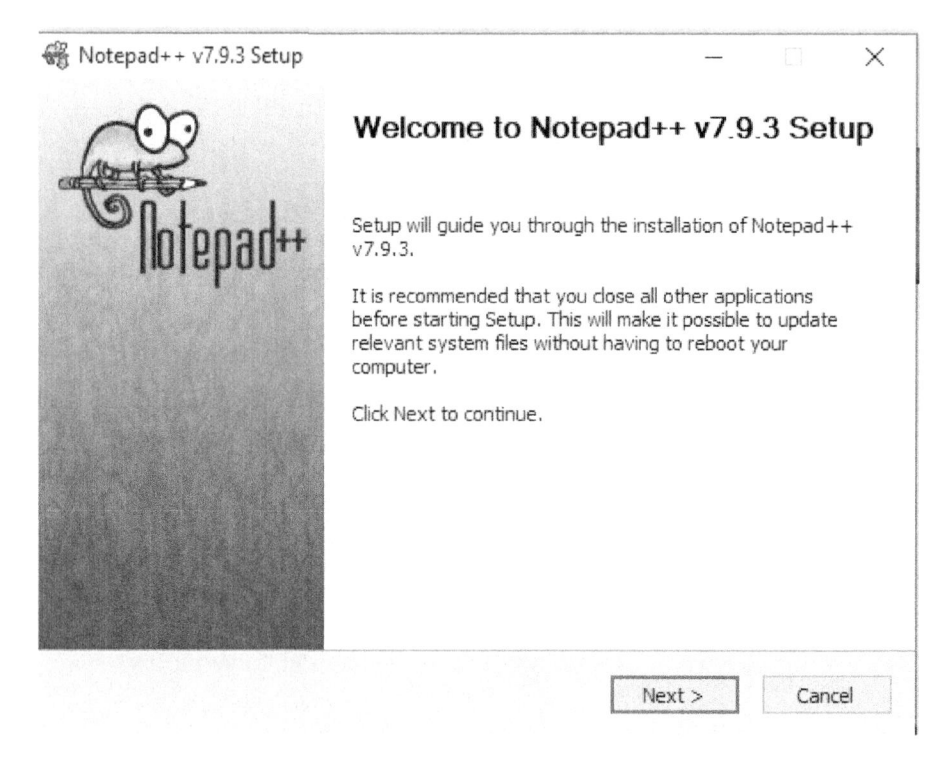

Welcome to Notepad++ v7.9.3 Setup

Setup will guide you through the installation of Notepad++ v7.9.3.

It is recommended that you close all other applications before starting Setup. This will make it possible to update relevant system files without having to reboot your computer.

Click Next to continue.

Tick the *Create Shortcut on Desktop* checkbox and Install

8

Choose Components

Choose which features of Notepad++ v7.9.3 you want to install.

☑ Create Shortcut on Desktop

Don't use %APPDATA%
Enable this option to make Notepad++ load/write the configuration files from/to its install directory. Check it if you use Notepad++ in a USB device.

Software is like sex: It's better when it's free

< Back | Install | Cancel

Completing Notepad++ v7.9.3 Setup

Notepad++ v7.9.3 has been installed on your computer.

Click Finish to close Setup.

☑ Run Notepad++ v7.9.3

< Back | Finish | Cancel

```
 C:\Program Files\Notepad++\change.log - Notepad++

File  Edit  Search  View  Encoding  Language  Settings  Tools  Macro  Run  Plugins  Window

change.log

 1   Notepad++ v7.9.3 Enhancements & bug-fixes:
 2
 3   1.  Discontinued support for Windows XP due to technical reasons
 4   2.  Upgrade Notepad++ License: update GPL version from v2 to v3.
 5   3.  Fix the regression of copying line data from search results.
 6   4.  Fix "Print Line Number" preference is ignored for printing r
 7   5.  Fix a regression in Chinese Simplified localization.
 8   6.  Fix dockable panels not being displayed regression due to mu
 9   7.  Make split-lines feature work again with multi-edge rightmos
10   8.  Enhance modern style file dialog for allowing UNIX style fil
11   9.  Use the modern browse folder dialog to get folder path.
12  10.  Improve option for setting save dialog filter to All Types.
13  11.  Add ability to delete entries from combo box history in Find
14  12.  Fix lost session issue on Windows reboot/shutdown.
15  13.  Add "save Folder as Workspace in session" option in save ses
16  14.  Make value dialog height accurate in any DPI.
17  15.  Fix issue that Switch-To-Panel keyboard shortcuts cannot be
18  16.  Fix a memory leak issue.
19  17.  Fix blurry display problem on an extended monitor.
20  18.  Fix incompatible plugin not being deleted issue.
21  19.  Synchronize GUP localization file (if available) with Notepa
22  20.  Enhance "No update" dialog with the download page link in th
23  21.  Fix NPPM_SETLINENUMBERWIDTHMODE API not working issue.
24
25  More fixes & implementations detail:
26  https://notepad-plus-plus.org/downloads/v7.9.3/
```

Notepad++ installed successfully.

Chapter 2: HTML

Before we start coding, let's create a new folder which will store all our HTML files.

- Right click on your desktop screen, click *New* -> *Folder*.

- Name the folder *HTML*

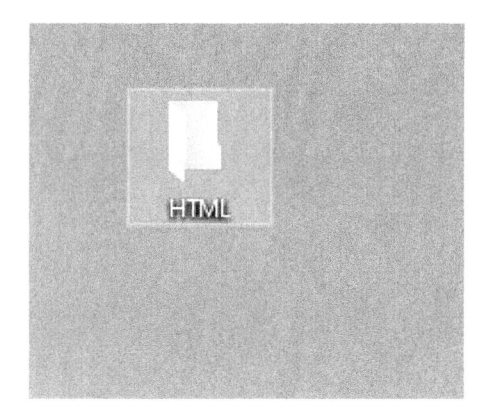

Now let's create our first HTML file and save it in the *HTML* folder.

- Open **Notepad++** -> Click on *File* -> *New*

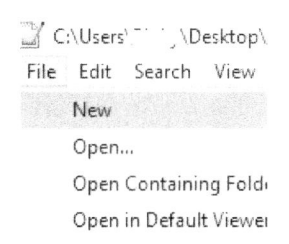

11

A new file is generated.

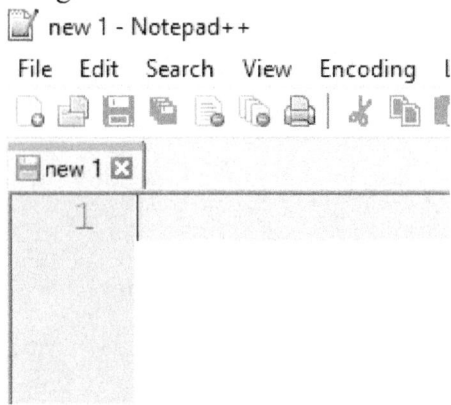

- Now let's convert this text file into an HTML document. Click on *File -> Save As*

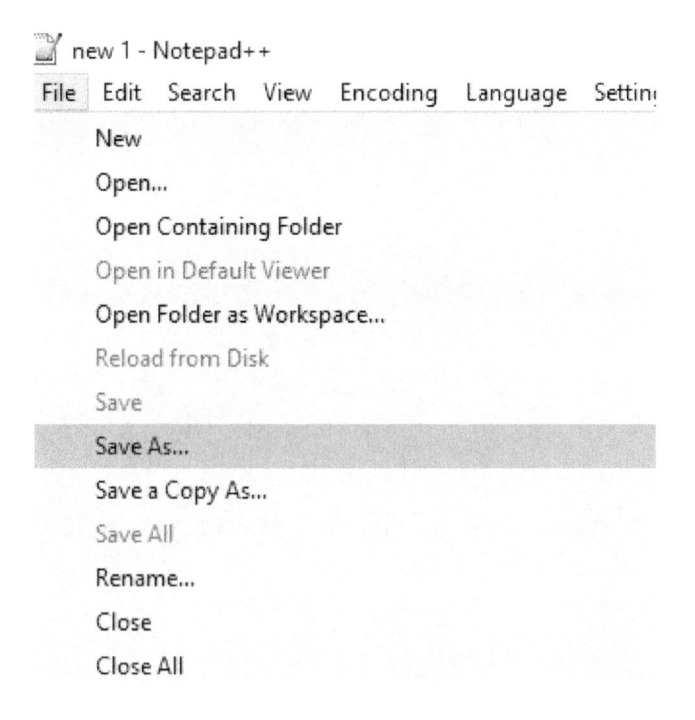

Give the *File name* (*I named hello*), in *Save as type* select **Hyper Test Markup Language file** and save it in the *HTML* folder created above.

> This PC > Desktop > HTML

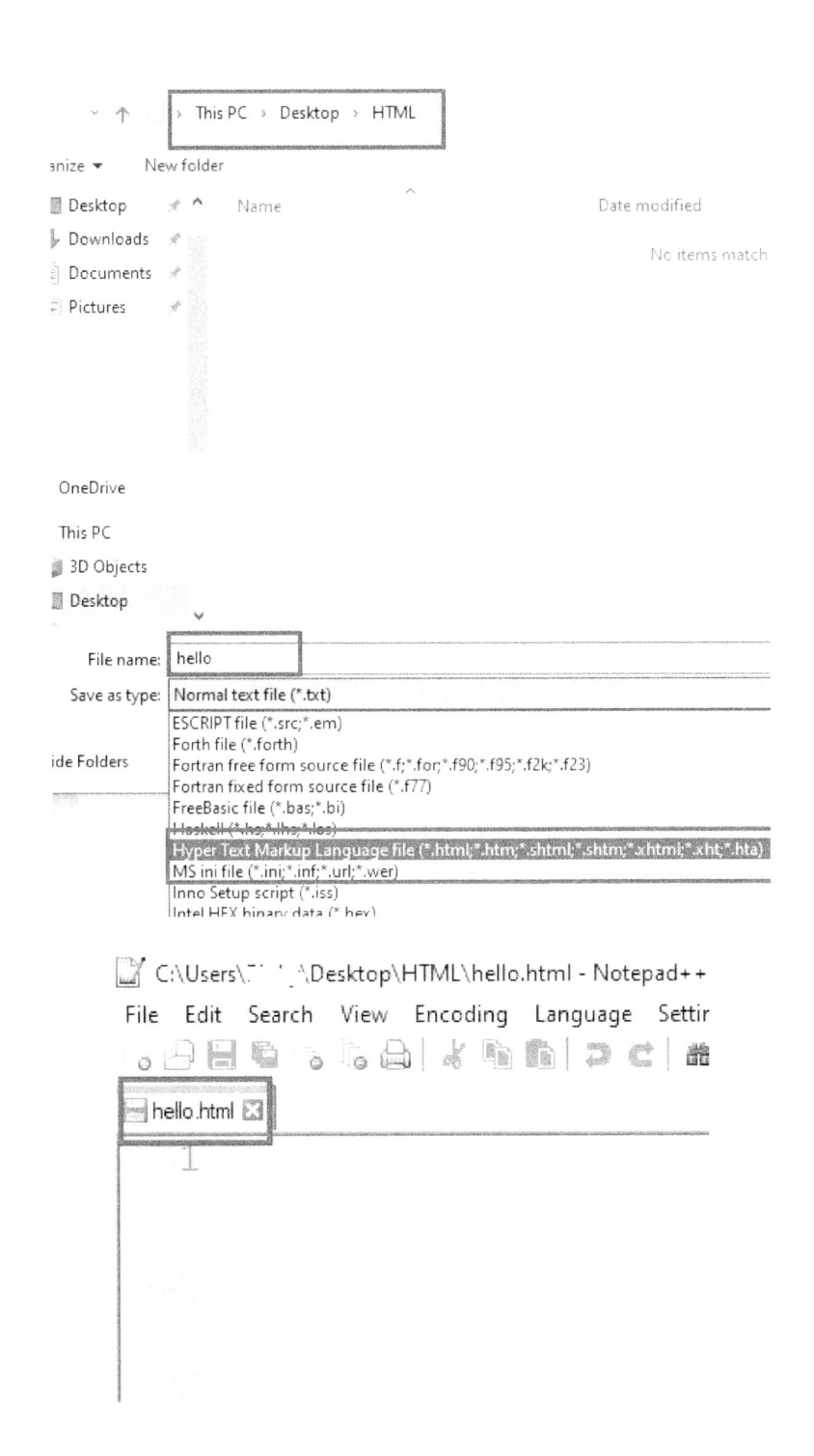

anize ▼   New folder

- Desktop
- Downloads
- Documents
- Pictures

Name   Date modified

No items match

OneDrive

This PC
- 3D Objects
- Desktop

File name: hello

Save as type: Normal text file (*.txt)

ESCRIPT file (*.src;*.em)
Forth file (*.forth)
Fortran free form source file (*.f;*.for;*.f90;*.f95;*.f2k;*.f23)
Fortran fixed form source file (*.f77)
FreeBasic file (*.bas;*.bi)
Haskell (*.hs;*.lhs;*.las)
Hyper Text Markup Language file (*.html;*.htm;*.shtml;*.shtm;*.xhtml;*.xht;*.hta)
MS ini file (*.ini;*.inf;*.url;*.wer)
Inno Setup script (*.iss)
Intel HEX binary data (*.hex)

C:\Users\...\Desktop\HTML\hello.html - Notepad++

File   Edit   Search   View   Encoding   Language   Settir

hello.html

13

In *hello.html* write the following lines of code.

```
<!DOCTYPE html>
<html>
    <head>
        <title>Hello World</title>
    </head>
    <body>
        Hello Kids
    </body>
</html>
```

Now let's run the above piece of code.

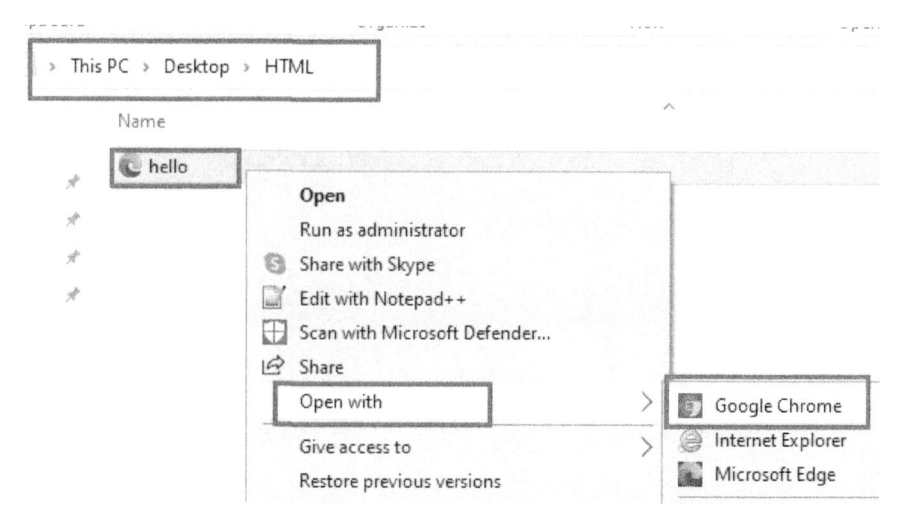

➤ Open the *HTML* folder -> right click on the *hello* HTML file -> click **Open with** -> select and click **Google Chrome** *(or any other browser you like)*.

14

We have successfully created our first web page.

2.1 : Headings

To set the heading of a web page, HTML provides us with **<h1>** to **<h6>** tag.

Open **Notepad++** -> open the existing *hello.html* file *(or create a new HTML file)* and write the following lines of code

```
<!DOCTYPE html>
<html>
    <head>
        <title>Hello World</title>
    </head>
    <body>
        <h1>Heading 1</h1>

        <h2>Heading 2</h2>

        <h3>Heading 3</h3>

        <h4>Heading 4</h4>

        <h5>Heading 5</h5>

        <h6>Heading 6</h6>
    </body>
</html>
```

Run the above piece of code.

➢ Refresh *hello.html* or open the *HTML* folder -> right click on the *hello* HTML file -> click **Open with** -> select and click **Google Chrome** *(or any other browser you like)*.

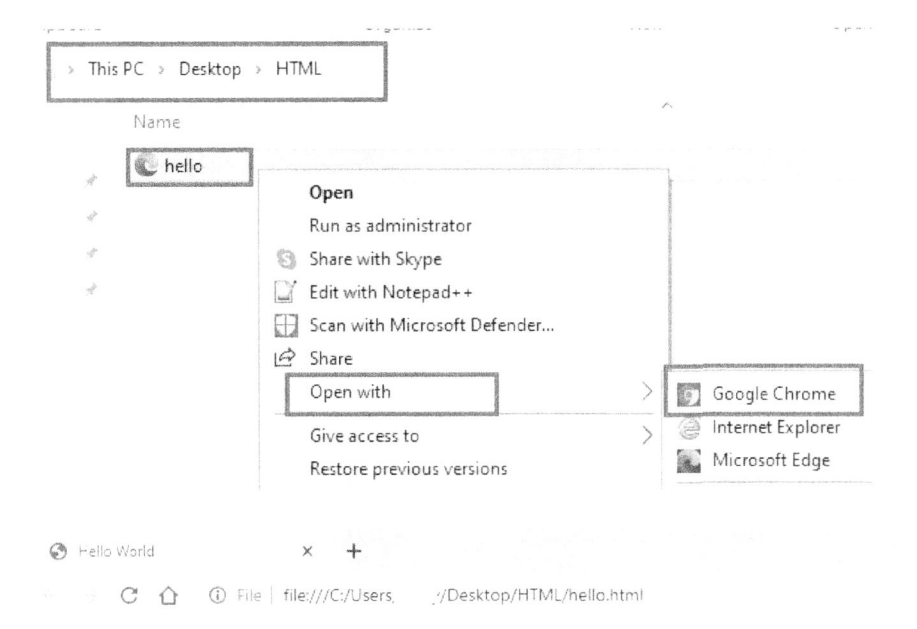

Heading 1

Heading 2

Heading 3

Heading 4

Heading 5

Heading 6

2.2 : Paragraph

In HTML, **<p>** tag is used to write a paragraph. The syntax is:

<p>
……..*text* ……….
</p>

Open **Notepad++** -> open the existing ***hello.html*** file *(or create a new HTML file)* and write a paragraph within the **<p>** tag as shown in the screen shot below.

```
hello.html
<!DOCTYPE html>
<html>
    <head>
        <title>Hello World</title>
    </head>
    <body>

    <p>

    Kind words are short, sweet and easy to speak
    but their echoes can truely last forever in someone's life

    </p>

    </body>
</html>
```

Run the above piece of code.

➢ Refresh ***hello.html*** or open the ***HTML*** folder -> right click on the ***hello*** HTML file -> click **Open with** -> select and click **Google Chrome** *(or any other browser you like).*

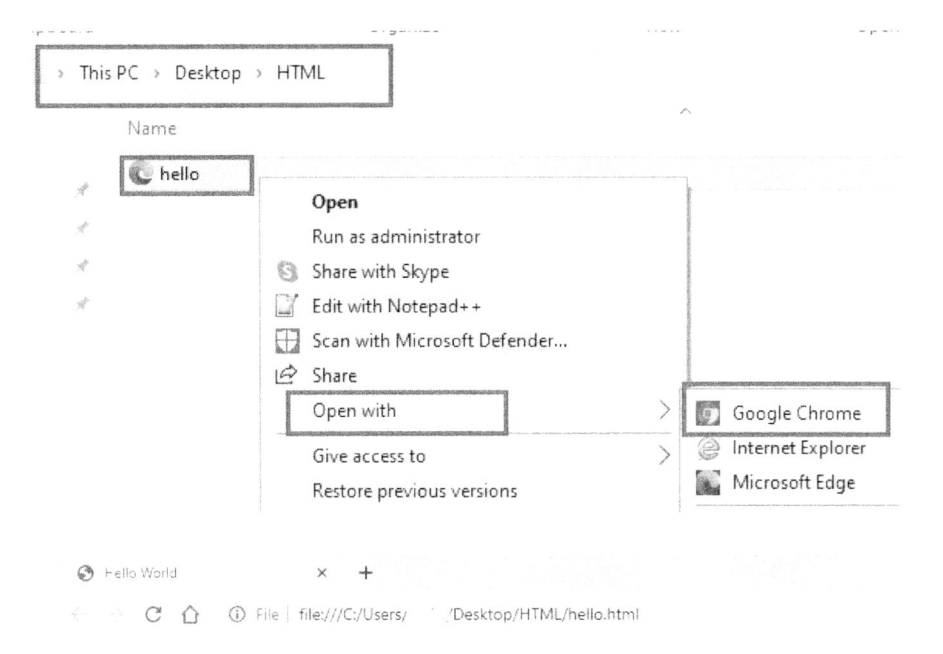

[Screenshot showing Windows File Explorer with a right-click context menu on "hello" file, with "Open with" submenu expanded showing Google Chrome, Internet Explorer, and Microsoft Edge options. Below is a browser window titled "Hello World" displaying the file path file:///C:/Users/.../Desktop/HTML/hello.html]

Kind words are short, sweet and easy to speak but their echoes can truely last forever in someone's life

2.3 : Links

- HTML links enable a user to go from one page to another.

- **<a>** tag is used to define a hyperlink or simply a link and its **href attribute** specifies the **url** of the page the link goes to.

The syntax for creating a link is:

<a href = *"......url......" > link_name* **</a>**

Open **Notepad++** -> open the existing **hello.html** file *(or create a new HTML file)* and write the following lines of code

```
<!DOCTYPE html>
<html>
    <head>
        <title>Hello World</title>
    </head>
    <body>

        <a href = "https://www.google.com/">
        Google website
        </a>

    </body>
</html>
```

Run the above piece of code.

➢ Refresh *hello.html* or open the *HTML* folder -> right click on the *hello* HTML file -> click **Open with** -> select and click **Google Chrome** *(or any other browser you like)*.

> This PC > Desktop > HTML

Name

hello

Open
Run as administrator
Share with Skype
Edit with Notepad++
Scan with Microsoft Defender...
Share
Open with   >   Google Chrome
Give access to   >   Internet Explorer
Restore previous versions   Microsoft Edge

Hello World   ×   +

← → C ⌂   ⓘ File | file:///C:/Users/_,/Desktop/HTML/hello.html

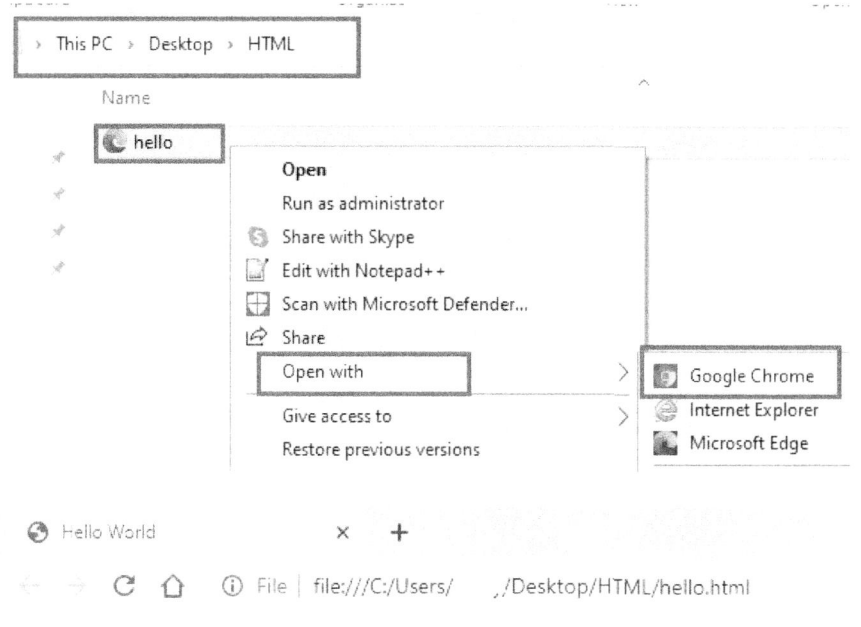

Google website

➢ Click on the link.

21

2.4 : Image

The syntax for adding any image into the web page is:

<img src = *"……image_location……"* **alt =** *"image_name"* **>**

- **src attribute** specifies the image location.

- **alt attribute** is used to set an alternate text for the image in case the image fails to load.

Let's download an image and save it in the *HTML* folder.

> This PC > Desktop > HTML

Name

hello

Scooby

*I downloaded an image of Scooby Do and saved it in **HTML** folder. It's a JPG file.*
The Scooby Do image location is C:\Users\...\Desktop\HTML and in order to access this image we can use its full path C:\Users\...\Desktop\HTML\Scooby.jpg.

Open **Notepad++** -> open the existing ***hello.html*** file *(or create a new HTML file)* and write the following lines of code.

```
hello.html
<!DOCTYPE html>
<html>
    <head>
        <title>Hello World</title>
    </head>
    <body>

        <img src = "C:\Users\  \Desktop\HTML\Scooby.jpg" alt = "scooby_pic">

    </body>
</html>
```

Run the above piece of code.

➢ Refresh ***hello.html*** or open the ***HTML*** folder -> right click on the ***hello*** HTML file -> click **Open with** -> select and click **Google Chrome** *(or any other browser you like).*

23

> This PC > Desktop > HTML

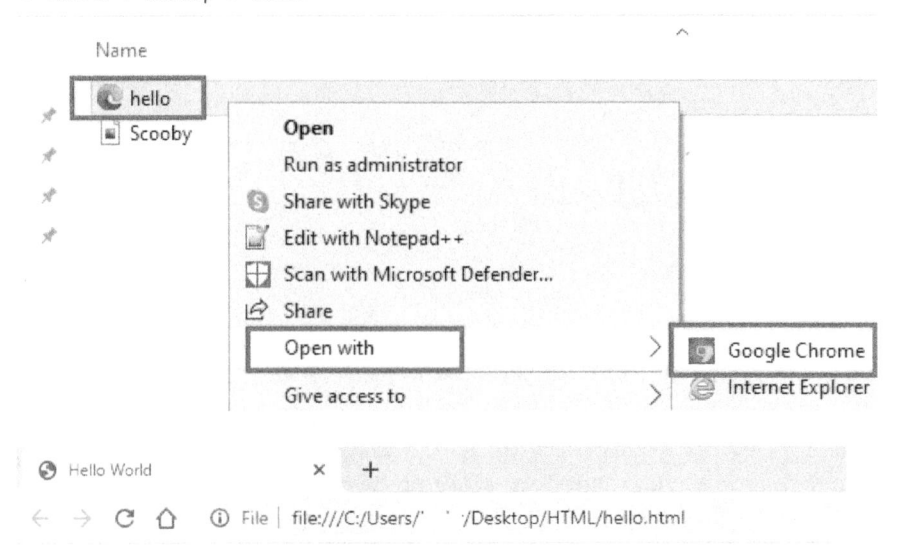

Name

🌙 hello
🖼 Scooby

Open
Open
Run as administrator
Share with Skype
Edit with Notepad++
Scan with Microsoft Defender...
Share
Open with   >   🟢 Google Chrome
Give access to   >   🅔 Internet Explorer

🌐 Hello World   ×   +

← → C ⌂   ⓘ File | file:///C:/Users/`  `/Desktop/HTML/hello.html

24

2.5 : Tables

Standard tables have rows, columns, headings and data as shown in the example below:

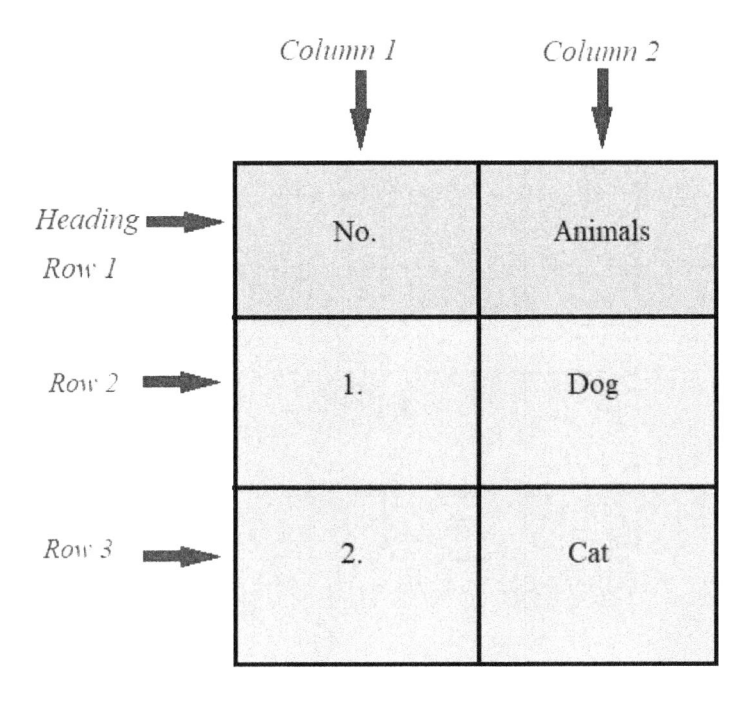

	No.	Animals
Heading Row 1		
Row 2	1.	Dog
Row 3	2.	Cat

Column 1 and *Column 2* are indicated above the No. and Animals columns respectively.

If we want to code the above table in HTML, we need tags like <table>, <th>, <tr> and <td>.

The syntax for creating a table is:

<table>
<th> ..... </th>
<tr> <td> .... </td></tr>
<tr> <td> .... </td></tr>
....
</table>

- <th> stands for table header

25

- **<tr>** stands for table row
- **<td>** stands for table data

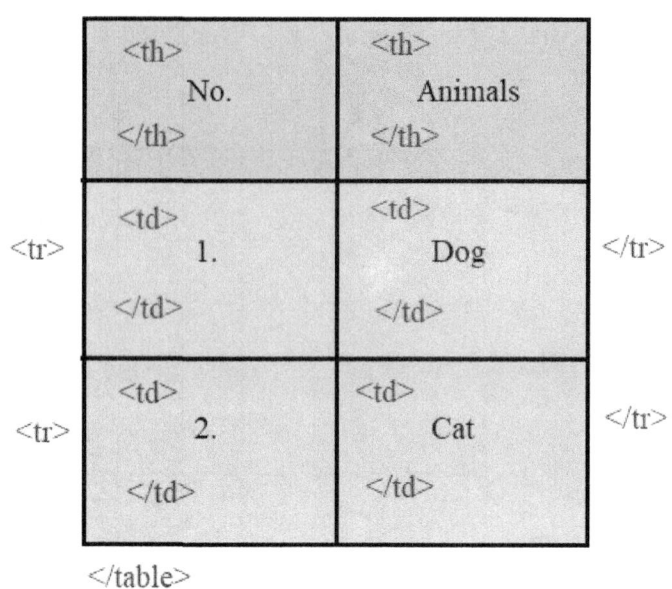

<table>

	<th> No. </th>	<th> Animals </th>	
<tr>	<td> 1. </td>	<td> Dog </td>	</tr>
<tr>	<td> 2. </td>	<td> Cat </td>	</tr>

</table>

Open **Notepad++** -> open the existing ***hello.html*** file *(or create a new HTML file)* and write the following lines of code.

```
<!DOCTYPE html>
<html>
    <head>
        <title>Hello World</title>
    </head>
    <body>

        <table>
            <th>No.</th>
            <th>Animals</th>

            <tr>
                <td>1.</td>
                <td>Dog</td>
            </tr>

            <tr>
                <td>2.</td>
                <td>Cat</td>
            </tr>
        </table>


    </body>
</html>
```

Run the above piece of code.

➢ Refresh *hello.html* or open the *HTML* folder -> right click on the *hello* HTML file -> click **Open with** -> select and click **Google Chrome** *(or any other browser you like).*

> This PC > Desktop > HTML

Name

- hello
- Scooby

Open
Run as administrator
Share with Skype
Edit with Notepad++
Scan with Microsoft Defender...
Share
Open with > Google Chrome
Give access to > Internet Explorer

🌐 Hello World   ×   +

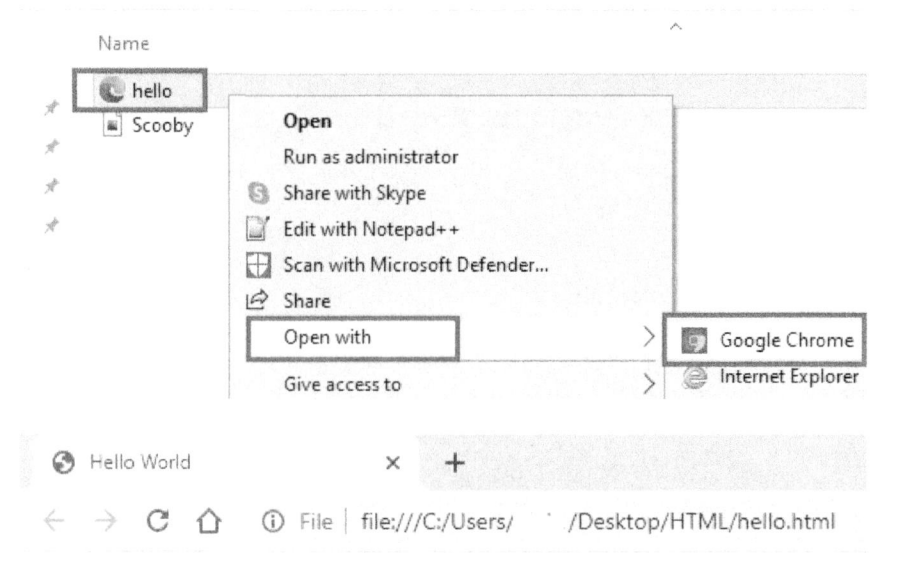

← → C ⌂   ⓘ File | file:///C:/Users/ /Desktop/HTML/hello.html

No. Animals
1. Dog
2. Cat

Please note: In order to add borders and make the table look pretty, we need CSS *(discussed in chapter 3)*.

28

2.6 : List

Important points to note are:
- In order to make a list of items HTML provide us with <ul>, <ol> and <li> tags.

- HTML List is divided into **unordered list** and **ordered list**.

- Syntax for creating **unordered list** is:

<ul>
<li> ....item 1 ..... </li>
<li> .....item 2 ...... </li>
</ul>

- Syntax for creating **ordered list** is:

<ol>
<li> .... item 1 ... </li>
<li> .....item 2 ..... </li>
</ol>

Open **Notepad++** -> open the existing *hello.html* file *(or create a new HTML file)* and write the following lines of code

```
hello.html
<!DOCTYPE html>
<html>
    <head>
        <title>Hello World</title>
    </head>
    <body>

     <ul>
        <li>Dog</li>
        <li>Cat</li>
     </ul>

     <ol>
        <li>Monkey</li>
        <li>Cow</li>
     </ol>

    </body>
</html>
```

Run the above piece of code.

➢ Refresh *hello.html* or open the *HTML* folder -> right click on the *hello* HTML file -> click **Open with** -> select and click **Google Chrome** *(or any other browser you like)*.

› This PC › Desktop › HTML

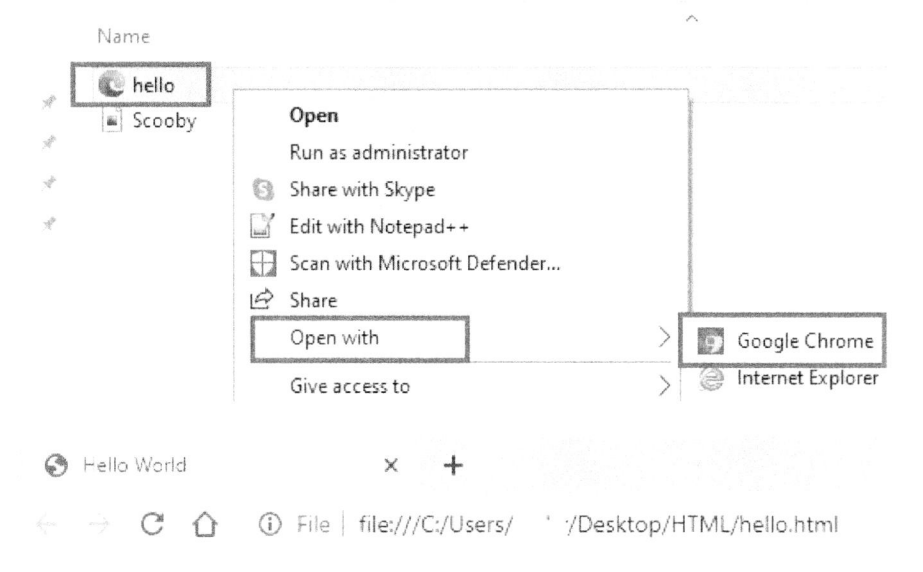

Name

- hello
- Scooby

Open
Open
Run as administrator
Share with Skype
Edit with Notepad++
Scan with Microsoft Defender...
Share
Open with   >   Google Chrome
Give access to >   Internet Explorer

🌐 Hello World   × +

← → C ⌂ ⓘ File | file:///C:/Users/ˈ /Desktop/HTML/hello.html

- Dog
- Cat

1. Monkey
2. Cow

2.7 : Drop Down Menu

The syntax for creating a drop down menu is:

<select>
<option value = *"value"* > *item 1* **</option>**
<option value = *"value"* > *item 2* **</option>**
.....
</select>

Open **Notepad++** -> open the existing *hello.html* file *(or create a new HTML file)* and write the following lines of code.

```
hello.html
<!DOCTYPE html>
<html>
    <head>
        <title>Hello World</title>
    </head>
    <body>

        <select>
            <option value = "dog">DOG</option>
            <option value = "cat">CAT</option>
            <option value = "lion">LION</option>
            <option value = "tiger">TIGER</option>
        </select>

    </body>
</html>
```

Run the above piece of code.

➢ Refresh *hello.html* or open the *HTML* folder -> right click on the *hello* HTML file -> click **Open with** -> select and click **Google Chrome** *(or any other browser you like).*

> This PC > Desktop > HTML

Name

- hello
- Scooby

Open
Run as administrator
Share with Skype
Edit with Notepad++
Scan with Microsoft Defender...
Share
Open with > Google Chrome
                Internet Explorer
Give access to >

Hello World   ×   +

← → C ⌂   ⓘ File | file:///C:/Users/....../Desktop/HTML/hello.html

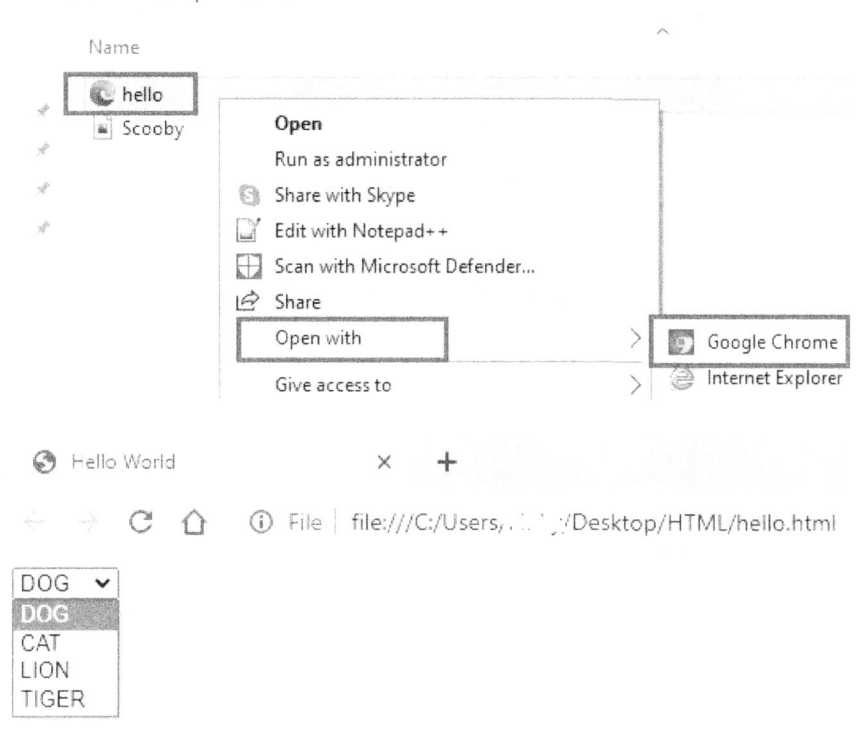

DOG ⌄
DOG
CAT
LION
TIGER

NOTE: The <u>first item</u> in the option within the **<select>** tag is always the default item which is displayed first when the page loads.

33

2.8 : Input tags

HTML **<input>** tag performs multiple functions based on the **type attribute**.

Most commonly used **input types** are:

1. The **<input>** syntax which will take only text value is:

<input type = "text"   placeholder = *"default_name "* >

2. The **<input>** syntax which will take only password value is:

<input type = "password"   placeholder = *"default_name "* >

3. The **<input>** syntax for submit button:

<input type = "submit" >

4. The **<input>** syntax for radio button:

<input type = "radio" >

5. The **<input>** syntax for checkbox:

<input type = "checkbox">

What is placeholder attribute?

Placeholder attribute is used to display a hint of what the text box expects from the user to enter.

Open **Notepad++** -> open the existing ***hello.html*** file *(or create a new HTML file)* and write the following lines of code.

```
<!DOCTYPE html>
<html>
    <head>
        <title>Hello World</title>
    </head>
    <body>

    Username <input type = "text" placeholder = "Enter username">

    <br><br>

    Password <input type = "password" placeholder = "Enter username">

    <br><br>

    Radio Button <input type = "radio">

    <br><br>

    <input type = "submit">

    </body>
</html>
```

Please note: `<br>` tag is the line break HTML element.

Run the above piece of code.

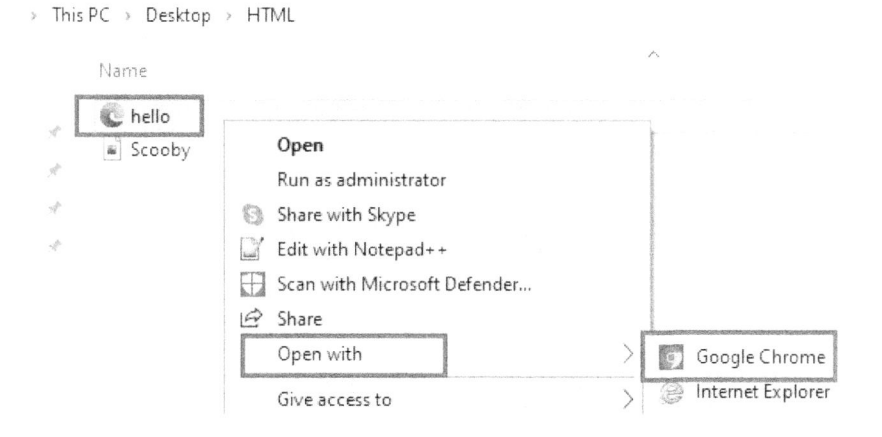

➢ Refresh *hello.html* or open the *HTML* folder -> right click on the *hello* HTML file -> click **Open with** -> select and click **Google Chrome** *(or any other browser you like)*.

> This PC > Desktop > HTML

Name
hello
Scooby

Open
- Run as administrator
- Share with Skype
- Edit with Notepad++
- Scan with Microsoft Defender...
- Share
- **Open with** > 🌐 Google Chrome
- Give access to > 🌐 Internet Explorer

35

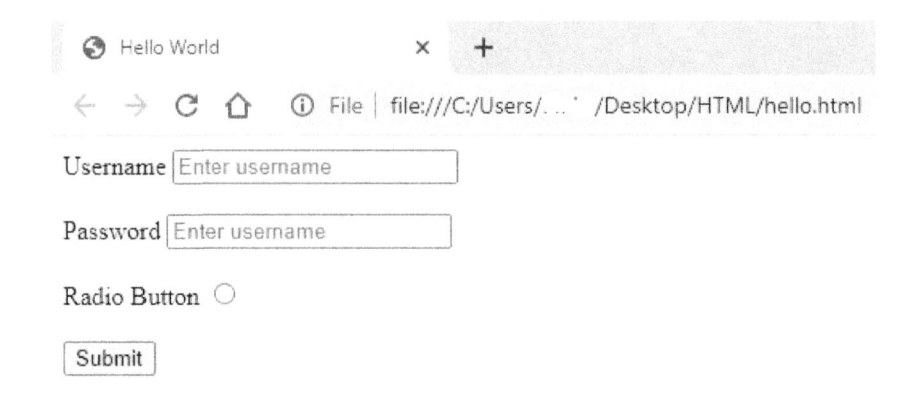

[Browser screenshot showing a form with Username field, Password field, Radio Button, and Submit button at URL file:///C:/Users/.../Desktop/HTML/hello.html]

2.9 : HTML Form

- The HTML **<form>** tag is used to create a HTML form where a user can enter data.

- The most important **attribute** of a **<form>** tag is its **action attribute**.

  The **action attribute** contains a **url** and once the form is submitted, the form data gets send to that specified **url**.

The syntax for creating a form is:
<form action = *"…url…"* **>**
….HTML input elements…
….
submit button
</form>

Let's create a new HTML file *(I named my file **user.html**)*

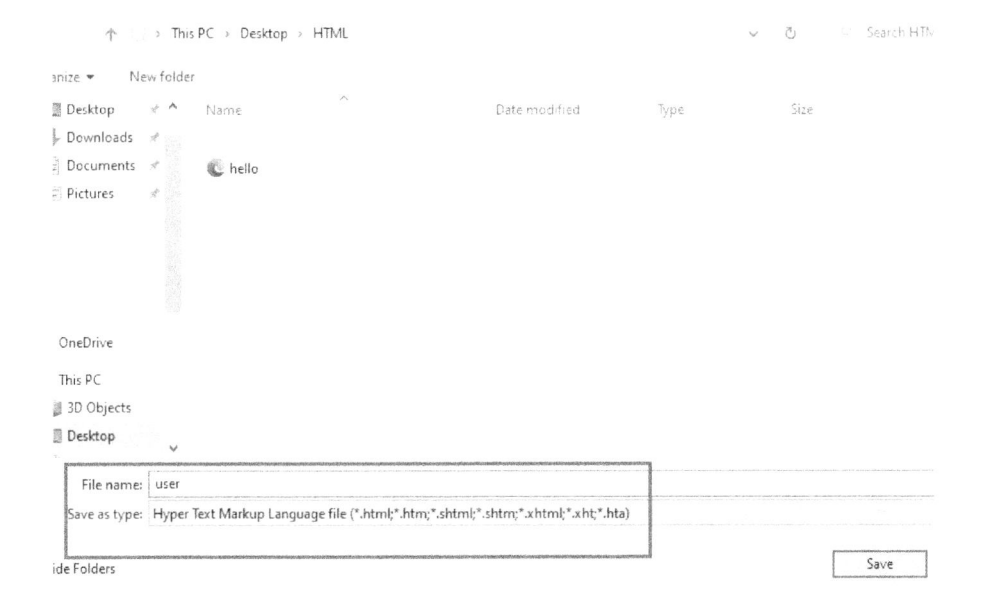

In ***user.html,*** I wrote few lines of code.

```
user.html
1  <!DOCTYPE html>
2  <html>
3      <head>
4          <title>User page</title>
5      </head>
6      <body>
7          Greetings........
8      </body>
9  </html>
10
```

Now open *hello.html* and create a simple HTML form.

```
hello.html
<!DOCTYPE html>
<html>
    <head>
        <title>Hello World</title>
    </head>
    <body>

        <form action = "user.html">

            <input type = "text" placeholder = "Enter Name">

            <br><br>

            <input type = "submit">

        </form>

    </body>
</html>
```

Please note: Since *user.html* and *hello.html* is present in the same folder, we do not have to give the full path *(C:\Users\....\Desktop\HTML\user.html)* in the **action attribute**. We can simply just write the file name.

38

> If *user.html* was present in some different folder, then we have to give its full path location.

Run the above piece of code.

➢ Refresh *hello.html* or open the *HTML* folder -> right click on the *hello* HTML file -> click **Open with** -> select and click **Google Chrome** *(or any other browser you like)*.

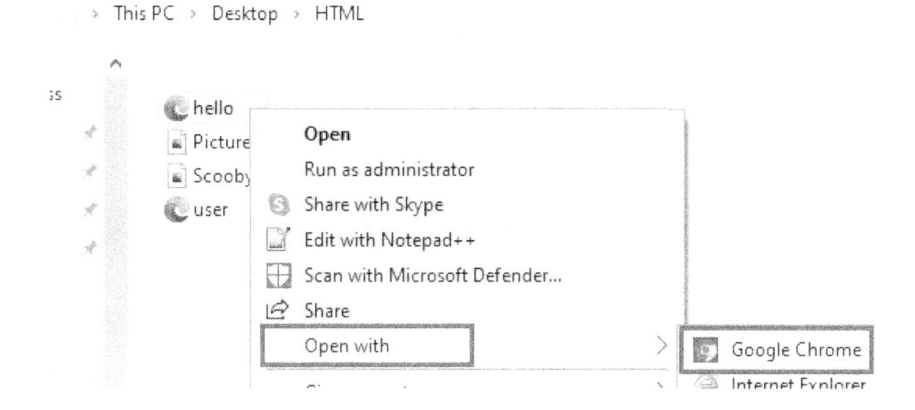

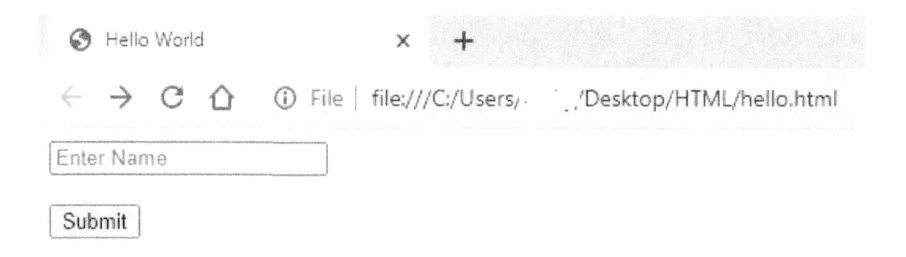

➢ Click on submit button and you will see *user.html* page shows up.

Greetings........

Chapter 3: CSS

CSS or Cascading Style Sheets is of three types:
1. Internal CSS
2. External CSS
3. Inline CSS

Commonly used CSS Properties

CSS Properties	Description
width	This property sets the width of the HTML **body**, containers and fields.
height	This property sets the height of the HTML **body**, containers and fields.
background - image	This property sets the background image of the HTML **body** or any container.
background-repeat	This property repeats the background image.

background-color	This property sets the background color of the HTML **body** or any container.
margin-left	The margin-left property sets the left margin of a HTML element or container.
margin-right	The margin-right property sets the right margin of a HTML element or container.
float	The CSS float property is used to place an element to the left or right of its parent container.
font-family	This property sets the font type of the text.
font-size	This property sets the font size of the text.
font-style	This property sets the font style (normal or italic) of the text.

font-weight	This CSS property is used to make a text bold or lighter.
color	This property sets the font color of the text.
text-align	This property aligns the text to the left, right or center of a container.
text-decoration	This property specifies the decoration added to the text.
border	This property sets the border around the table or any container.
border-left	This property sets the left border of the table or any container.
border-right	This property sets the right border of the table or any container.

border-bottom	This property sets the bottom border of the table or any container.
border-top	This property sets the top border of the table or any container.
border-color	This property sets the border color of the table or any container.
position	*Position properties explained in section 3.1.4*
top	*Position properties explained in section 3.1.4*
bottom	*Position properties explained in section 3.1.4*
left	*Position properties explained in section 3.1.4*
right	*Position properties explained in section 3.1.4*

The above CSS properties are the most important and commonly used ones. To learn about additional CSS properties, please visit website **https://www.w3schools.com/**

3.1 : Internal CSS

- In Internal CSS, the CSS code and the HTML code are present within the same HTML document.

- The CSS codes are written within **<style>** tags in the **<head>** section of a HTML file.

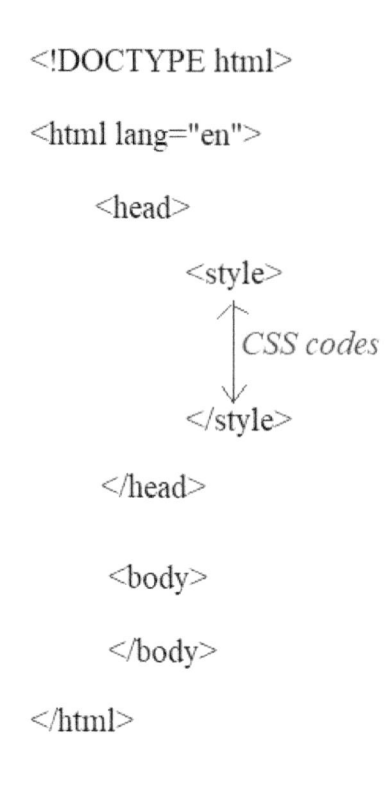

```
<!DOCTYPE html>
<html lang="en">
    <head>
        <style>
            ↑
            │ CSS codes
            ↓
        </style>
    </head>
    <body>
    </body>
</html>
```

- To add CSS styling information to the web page, we have to call each HTML element within the **<style>** tag by its **name** or by its **ID** or by its **Class** name. *(we will learn about CSS **ID** and **Class** with examples as we proceed further)* and provide CSS code.

```
<style>

    HTML element name {

        ....... CSS code.....

    }

</style>
```

Example:

Let's create a web page on **Dogs**. Download a few of your favorite pictures of Dog and let's get started.

Open **Notepad++** -> create a new file -> save as HTML document and store it in the ***HTML*** folder *(created in chapter 2)*.
*I named my file **dogs.html**.*

3.1.1 : Add a background image to the web page

```html
<!DOCTYPE html>
<html>
    <head>
        <title>Dogs</title>

        <style>

          body{
             background-image: url("Picture4.jpg");
             background-repeat:repeat;
          }

        </style>
    </head>

    <body>

    </body>
</html>
```

The following styling information is provided to the **body** of the web page:

- o To add a background image, the CSS code is:

    background - image : url (" *picture_location* **") ;**

> **Please note:** Since *dogs.html* and *Picture4.jpg* are present in the same folder, we do not have to give the full path (*C:\Users\.....\Desktop\HTML\Picture4.jpg*). The code will run fine if we simply give the image name in the **url** location.

- o If you want the background image to **repeat** itself and fill the web page then the CSS code is:

    background-repeat : repeat;

Additional Information:

1. If you want the background image to repeat itself vertically, the syntax is:
background-repeat : repeat-y

2. If you want the background image to repeat itself horizontally, the syntax is:
background-repeat : repeat-x

Run the above piece of code.

➢ Open the *HTML* folder -> right click on the *dogs* HTML file -> click **Open with** -> select and click **Google Chrome** *(or any other browser you like).*

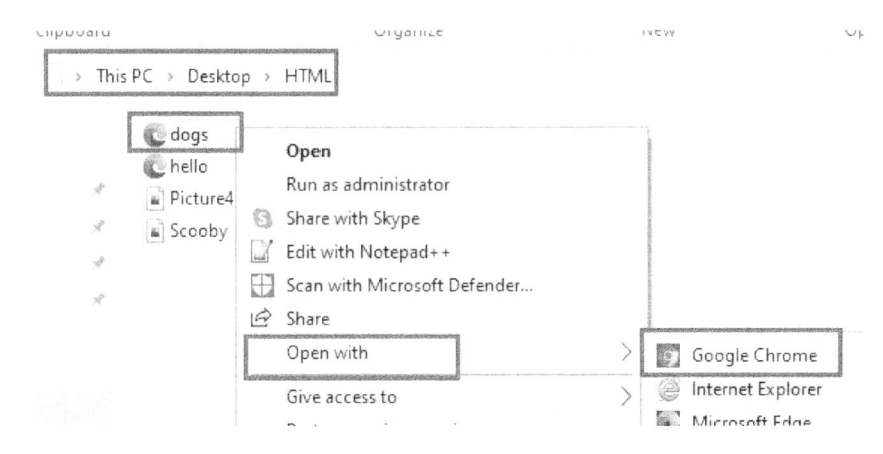

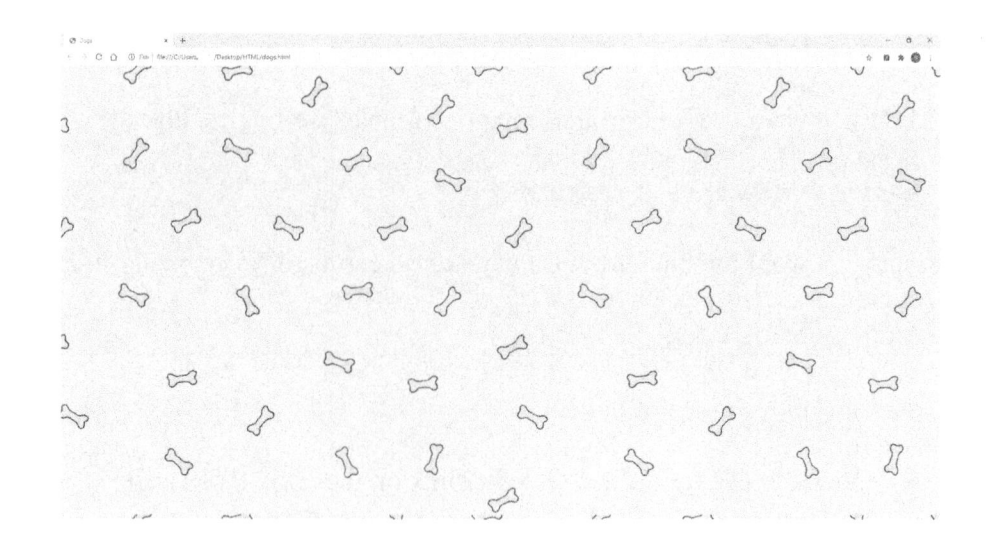

3.1.2 : Set a height and width

It is very important to set the height and width of the **body**, containers and fields of a web page.

The CSS code for adding height and width is:

width : *a number is percentage or pixel (px)*
height: *a number is percentage or pixel (px)*

In ***dogs.html***, add the highlighted lines of code shown in the screen shot below.

```
<style>
body{
  background-image: url("Picture4.jpg");
  background-repeat:repeat;
  width:100%;
  height:100%;
}
</style>
```

Please note: Always remember to set the height and width of the **body** of a web page. It is because the **body** of a web page acts as a parent container and helps to prevent layout shifts of different elements present within the web page.

3.1.3 : Add a Heading

Let's create a separate section or division or container in our web page which will hold the heading.

NOTE: To create a division or a section or a container in our HTML document <**div**> tag is used.
The syntax is:
<**div**>
 ......
</**div**>

In *dogs.html*, write the following lines of code highlighted in the screen shot below.

51

```html
<!DOCTYPE html>
<html>
    <head>
        <title>Dogs</title>
        <style>
          body{
             background-image: url("Picture4.jpg");
             background-repeat:repeat;
             width:100%;
             height:100%;
          }

          #heading{
             width: 50%;
             height: 200px;
             background-color: white;
             margin-left:auto;
             margin-right:auto;
          }

          h1{
             font-family:Comic Sans MS;
             font-size:100px;
             color: orange;
             text-align:center;
          }
        </style>
    </head>

    <body>

        <div id = "heading">
            <h1>Dogs</h1>
        </div>

    </body>
</html>
```

Code explanation:

o   At line 32, we initiated a container with the help of **<div>** tag and this container will hold the heading of our web page. We assigned an **ID** name *heading* to the container.

What is ID in CSS?

ID helps to <u>uniquely</u> identify certain HTML elements. In order to access the **id** of an HTML element within **<style>** tag, a hashtag (#) symbol is used. Example: # *id_name*

```
<style>

        #ID name {

        ....... CSS code.....

        }

</style>
```

- o To add styling information to this container, we access the **ID** *heading* within the **<style>** tag and the following CSS code is provided to it:

    - ➢ **width:** 50%   *(We set the width of the container to 50%).*

    - ➢ **height:** 200px   *(We set the height of the container to 200px).*

    - ➢ **background-color :** white   *(We set the background color of the container to white).*

    - ➢ To align the container to the center of the page, we set the **margin-left** property to *auto* and **margin-right** property to *auto*.

- o This container holds the heading and the heading is written using <h1> tag.

The following styling information is added to the text written within the <h1> tag:

- **font-family:** Comic Sans MS *(We set its font type to Comic Sans MS).*

- **font-size:** 100px *(We set its font size to 100px).*

- **color:** orange *(We set the text color to orange).*

- **text-align:** center *(We aligned the text to the center of its parent container).*

Additional Information:

1. The CSS property used to make a text look bolder or lighter is:
font-weight : bold
or
font-weight : lighter

2. The CSS property used to add any style to the text is:
font-style: normal
or
font-style: italic

Run the above piece of code.

- Refresh *dogs.html* or open the *HTML* folder -> right click on the *dogs* HTML file -> click **Open with** -> select and click **Google Chrome** *(or any other browser you like).*

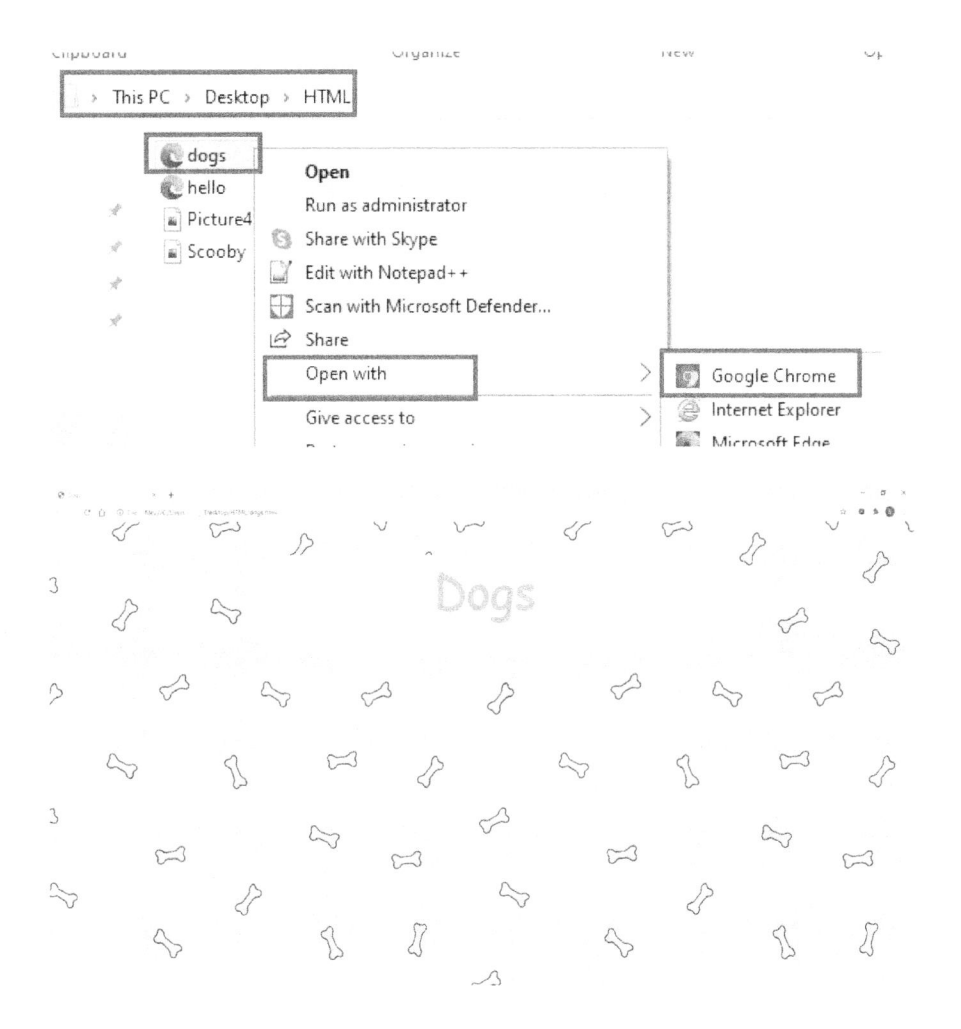

Let's summarize the process entire process:

1. We created a container with the help of HTML **<div>** tag. We gave an **ID** name *heading* to the container. This container will act as a parent container which will hold the **<h1>** tag.

```
<div id = "heading ">        //start parent container

    <h1>
    
    ..........
    
    </h1>

</div>                       //end parent container
```

2. To add styling information to the container, we called its **ID** name within the **<style>** tag and added a few lines of CSS code into it.

3. To add styling information to the heading, we called its name and added a few lines of CSS code into it.

> **Please Note:** While coding, it is a good practice to divide the web page into different divisions or sections or containers and store individual functionality of the web page in those containers.

3.1.4 : Add a list of link

In chapter 2, we learnt about **links** and **list**. In this section we will create a **list** of **links**.

In *dogs.html*, create another parent container.

```
19          }
20
21          h1{
22              font-family:Comic Sans MS;
23              font-size:100px;
24              color: orange;
25              text-align:center;
26          }
27
28          #main{
29              width: 100%;
30              height: 600px;
31              background-color: orange;
32              position:relative;
33          }
34      </style>
35   </head>
36
37   <body>
38
39      <div id = "heading">
40          <h1>Dogs</h1>
41      </div>
42
43      <div id = "main">
44
45
46      </div>
47
48   </body>
49 </html>
```

I gave the parent container an **ID** name ***main** (ID discussed in section 3.1.3)* and gave the styling information highlighted in the screen shot above.

> I set the width and height of the container using **width** and **height** CSS property. Then we assigned a background color to the parent container using **background-color** CSS property.

57

In the above CSS code, you will notice a new line:
position: relative

What is position property in CSS?

CSS position property helps to position an element to the **top, bottom, left** or **right** of the web page.

Suppose we want to position an element *x* to the top right corner of a container. In order to do this, we need to create a parent container and set its **position** property to **relative**. Then we need to set the **position** property of the child element *x* to **absolute** *(it is positioned relative to its parent container)*. After this we can position the child element *x* to the top right corner of its parent container using **top** and **right** CSS properties.

Let's create a child container within its parent container *(with **ID** main)* and this child container will hold the **list** of **links**.

```
#main{
    width: 100%;
    height: 600px;
    background-color: orange;
    position:relative;
}

#child_link_list{
    position:absolute;
    top:0px;
    right:20px;
    background-color: red;
    width:500px;
    height:50px;
}
        </style>
    </head>

    <body>

        <div id = "heading">
            <h1>Dogs</h1>
        </div>

        <div id = "main">

            <div id = "child_link_list">

            </div>

        </div>

    </body>
</html>
```

I gave the child container an **ID** name ***child_link_list*** and added the following styling information highlighted in the screen shot above.

> **position: absolute**

> **top:** 0px *(we set the top of the child container to 0px).*

59

- **right:** 20px *(we set the right side of the child container to 20px).*

- We assigned a background color to the child container using **background-color** CSS property and set the width and height of the container using **width** and **height** CSS property.

We have successfully created our parent container and child container. Now let's create the **list** of **links** within the child container.

```
            width:500px;
            height:50px;
      }
      li{
         display:inline;
         text-decoration:none;
      }
      a{
         padding:8px;
         color:orange;
         font-size:20px;
         font-family:Comic Sans MS;
         background-color:white;
      }
    </style>
</head>

<body>

 <div id = "heading">
      <h1>Dogs</h1>
 </div>

 <div id = "main">

   <div id = "child_link_list">
    <ul>
       <li><a href = "https://www.google.com/">Google</a></li>
       <li><a href = "https://www.yahoo.com/">Yahoo</a></li>
       <li><a href = "https://www.facebook.com/">Facebook</a></li>
       <li><a href = "https://www.amazon.com/">Amazon</a></li>
       <li><a href = "https://www.ebay.com/">Ebay</a></li>
    </ul>
   </div>
```

We created an **unordered list** using <ul> and <li> tag and then added the **links** using <a> tag *(these tags were discussed in chapter 2)*.

CSS code assigned to <li> tag

As you may recall, **unordered list** items are displayed with bullet points like the example below:
- item1
- item2
- ……

In ***dogs.html***, we would like to display the list items side by side and without any bullet points like the example below:
item1   item2   item3   …….

In order to do display the list items side by side and without any bullet points, we used the following CSS codes:

> ➢ **display: inline** *(This line of code will display the list items side by side).*

> ➢ **text-decoration : none** *(This line of code will not display any bullet points)*

CSS code assigned to <a> tag

In the styling information assigned to <a> tag, you will notice a new line of code:

> ➢ **padding:8px**

What is padding property?

Padding property is used to set padding around the text written within a HTML element.

61

➢ We set the *color, font size, font type* and *background color* of the text written within the <a> tag using **color, font-size, font-family, background-color** CSS properties.

Run the above piece of code..
➢ Refresh ***dogs.html*** or open the ***HTML*** folder -> right click on the ***dogs*** HTML file -> click **Open with** -> select and click **Google Chrome** *(or any other browser you like)*.

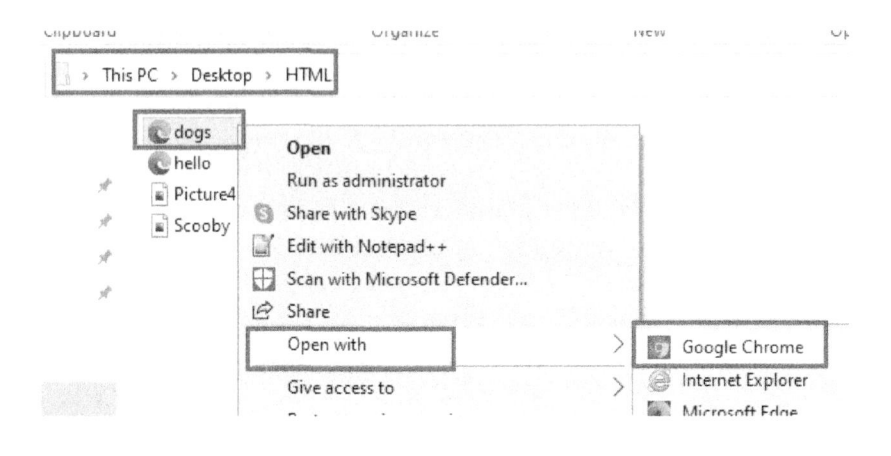

Everything works perfectly.

Now suppose you wish to change the background color of each link item or element, when a user hovers the mouse over it. In order to do that CSS **hover selector** is used.

The syntax is:
HTML element name : **hover** {
……*CSS code*…….
}

```
      }
      a{
        padding:8px;
        color:orange;
        font-size:20px;
        font-family:Comic Sans MS;
        background-color:white;
      }
      a:hover{
        background-color:gray;
      }
    </style>
  </head>

  <body>

    <div id = "heading">
        <h1>Dogs</h1>
    </div>

    <div id = "main">

      <div id = "child_link_list">

      <ul>
          <li><a href = "https://www.google.com/">Google</a></li>
          <li><a href = "https://www.yahoo.com/">Yahoo</a></li>
          <li><a href = "https://www.facebook.com/">Facebook</a></li>
          <li><a href = "https://www.amazon.com/">Amazon</a></li>
          <li><a href = "https://www.ebay.com/">Ebay</a></li>

      </ul>
```

Run the above piece of code..

> ➤ Refresh *dogs.html* or open the *HTML* folder -> right click on the *dogs* HTML file -> click **Open with** -> select and click **Google Chrome** *(or any other browser you like).*

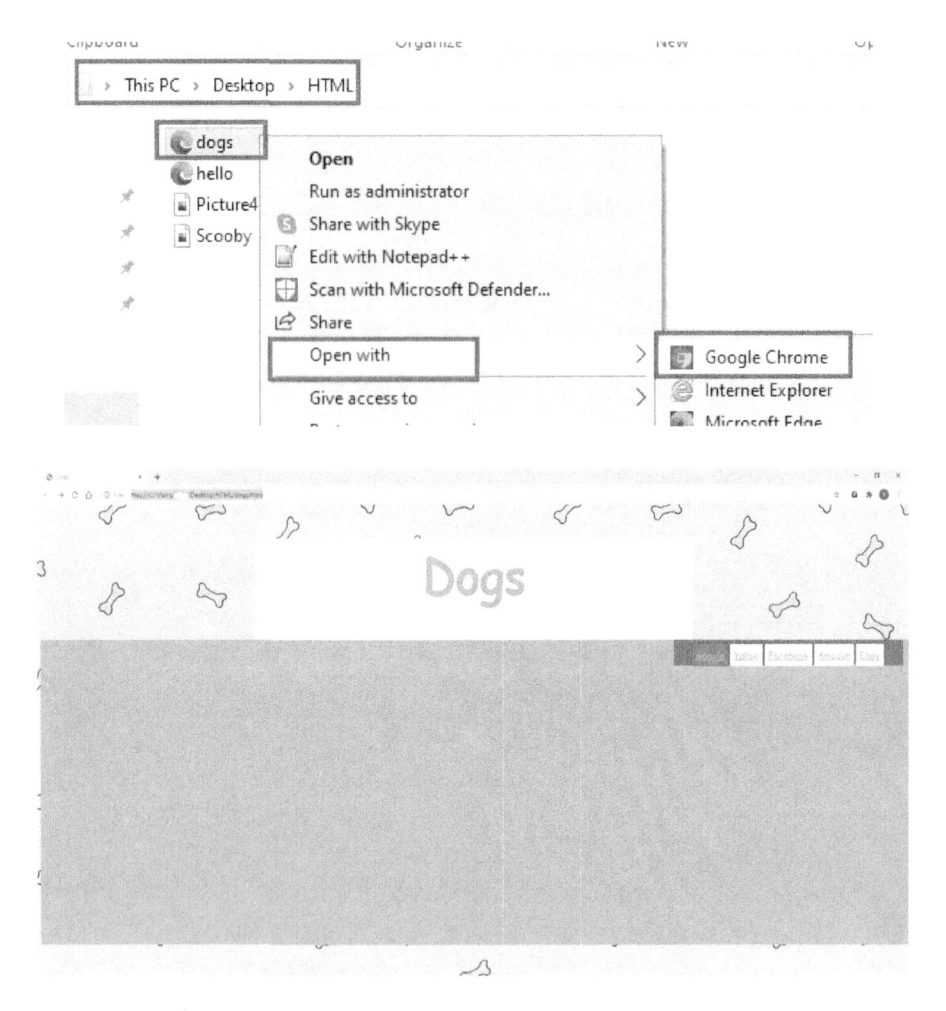

Let's summarize the above process:

1. We created a parent container and assigned it an **ID** name ***main***.

2. We created a child container within the parent container and assigned it an **ID** name ***child_link_list.***

```
<div id = "main">           //start parent container

<div id = "child_link_list">   //start child container

....list of links.....

</div>                      //end child container

</div>                      //end parent container
```

3. The child container is positioned to the top right corner of its parent container *(shown in the screen shot below as **child container 1**)* and the positioning was done with the help of CSS **position properties**.

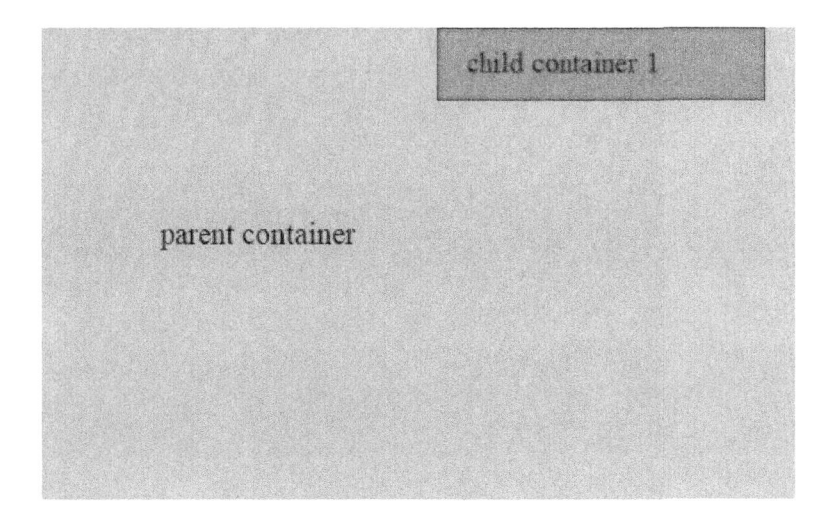

4. The child container contains the list of links.

> **Additional Information:**
>
> **What is CSS float property?**
>
> The CSS float property is used to place an element to the left or right of its parent container.
>
> Syntax:
> **float: left**
>
> or
>
> **float: right**

3.1.5 : Add a table

Let's create a another container with the help of **<div>** tag and this container will act as an child container to the parent container with **ID *main*** *(created in section 3.1.4)*

```
<div id = "main">

   <div id = "child_link_list">

   <ul>
        <li><a href = "https://www.goog
        <li><a href = "https://www.yaho
        <li><a href = "https://www.face
        <li><a href = "https://www.amaz
        <li><a href = "https://www.ebay

   </ul>
   </div>
   <div id = "table_container">



   </div>
```

I assigned an **ID** name *table_container (ID discussed in section 3.1.3)* to the child container highlighted in the screen shot above. The styling information assigned to the child container with **ID** *table_container* is:

```
#table_container{
      position:absolute;
      top:50px;
      left:33%;
}
```

position properties discussed in section 3.1.4

Now let's create the table within this container.

67

```html
        </div>

        <div id = "table_container">

        <table>
           <th>No.</th>
           <th>Breed</th>
           <th>Normal Weight</th>

           <tr>
           <td>1</td>
           <td>Labrador</td>
           <td>50-100lbs</td>
           </tr>

           <tr>
           <td>2</td>
           <td>American Bulldog</td>
           <td>60-100lbs</td>
           </tr>

            <tr>
           <td>3</td>
           <td>German Shepherd</td>
           <td>50-100lbs</td>
           </tr>

           <tr>
           <td>4</td>
           <td>Beagle</td>
           <td>20-50lbs</td>
           </tr>

        </table>

        </div>
```

This table will appear without any borders. To add border and some additional styling information the following CSS code is used:

```
table,td,th{
     border: 1px solid black;
     border-collapse: collapse;
}

td,th{
     padding: 20px;
     font-size:30px;
     font-family:Comic Sans MS;
}
```

> **border** : 1 px **solid** black *(This CSS code adds 1 px **solid** line border around the table, around each <td> data element and around each <th> header element).*

Additional Information:

Lines can be **solid, dotted** or **double**. For example:

border : 2 px **solid** orange
or
border : 2 px **dotted** orange
or
border : **double** orange

> **border-collapse: collapse** *(This CSS code collapses all the borders and form a single border).*

> We set the *padding* around each data element *(<td>)* and heading *(<th>)* with the help of **padding** property and set the *font size* and *font type* using **font-size** and **font-family** property.

Run the above piece of code..
> Refresh *dogs.html* or open the *HTML* folder -> right click on the *dogs* HTML file -> click **Open with** -> select and click **Google Chrome** *(or any other browser you like)*.

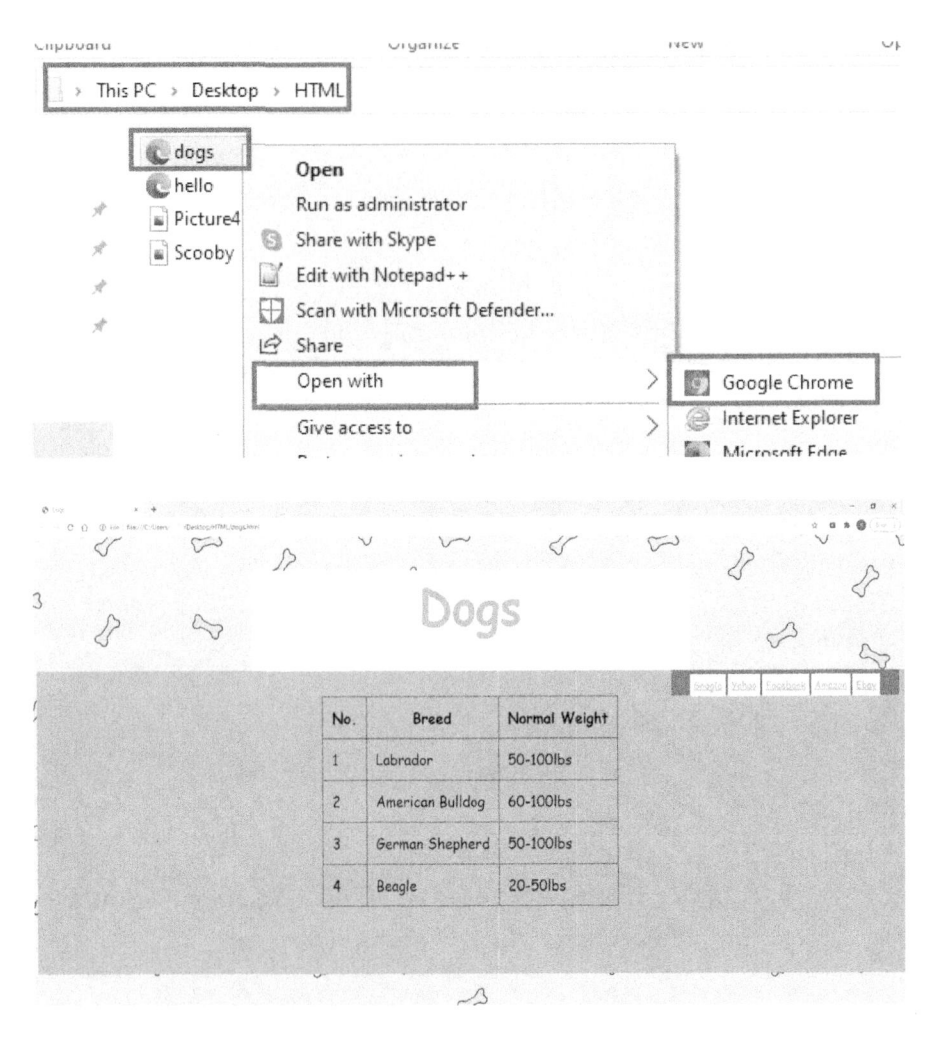

Let's summarize the above process:

1. We already have our parent container *(with **ID main**)* which we created in section 3.1.4.

2. We created a new child container and gave an **ID** name *table_container (highlighted in the screen shot below)*.

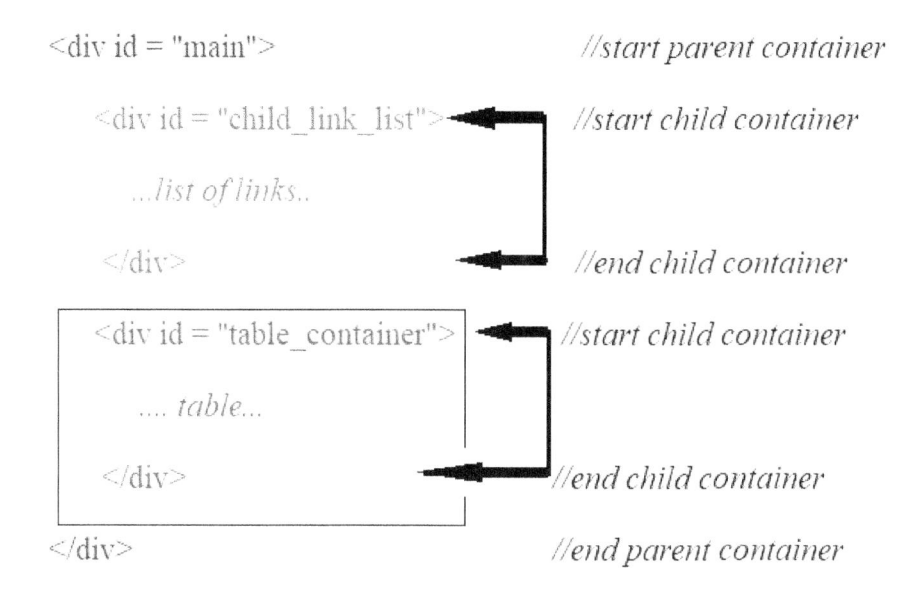

```
<div id = "main">                          //start parent container
    <div id = "child_link_list">           //start child container
        ...list of links..
    </div>                                 //end child container

    <div id = "table_container">           //start child container
        .... table...
    </div>                                 //end child container
</div>                                     //end parent container
```

3. I positioned the child container almost to the center of the screen *(shown in the screen shot below as **child container 2)** using **position properties**.

[Diagram: parent container containing "child container 1" and "child container 2"]

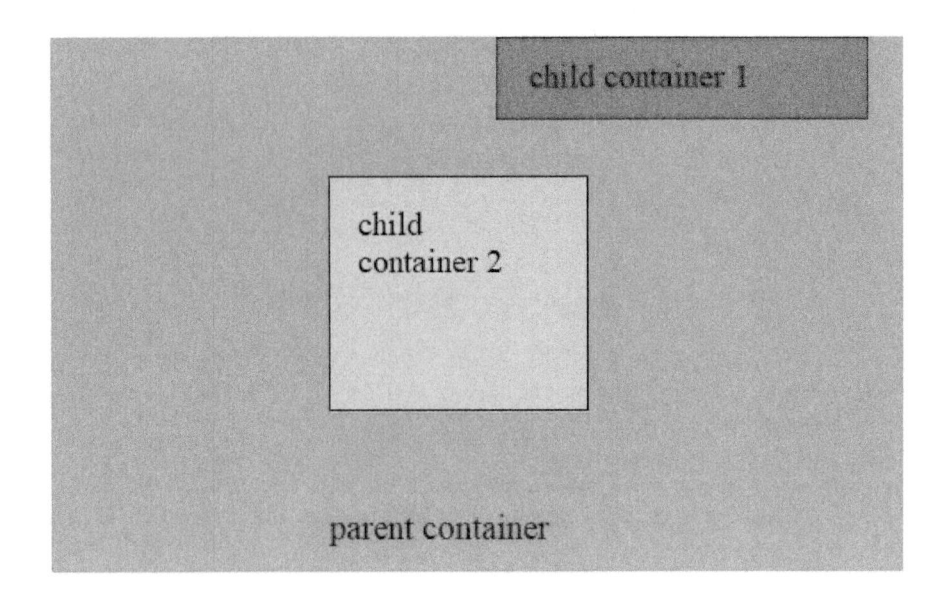

4. The child container contains the table.

3.1.6 : Add a drop down menu

Let's create another child container which will reside within the parent container with **ID *main*** *(created in section 3.1.4)* and this child container will hold the drop down menu.

```
        </tr>

         <tr>
         <td>3</td>
         <td>German Shepherd</td>
         <td>50-100lbs</td>
         </tr>

         <tr>
         <td>4</td>
         <td>Beagle</td>
         <td>20-50lbs</td>
         </tr>

    </table>

    </div>
```

```
<div id = "drop_down">



</div>
```

I gave the child container an **ID** name ***drop_down*** *(ID discussed in section 3.1.3)* as shown in the screen shot above. The CSS code assigned to the child container is:

```
#drop_down{
      position:absolute;
      top:0px;
      left:20px;
}
```

position property discussed in section 3.1.4.

73

Let's create the drop down menu within the child container.

```html
<div id = "drop_down">

    <select class = "optionVal">
        <option class = "optionVal" value = "dog_food">DOG FOOD LIST</option>
        <option class = "optionVal" value = "pedigree">Pedigree</option>
        <option class = "optionVal" value = "purina">Purina</option>
        <option class = "optionVal" value = "iams">Iams</option>
        <option class = "optionVal" value = "kirkland_signature">Kirkland Signature</option>
    </select>

</div>
```

From the above piece of code, you will notice the HTML elements <select> and <option> belong to **class** *optionVal*.

What is the difference between ID and Class in CSS?

1. A **class** selector is a name preceded by a full stop (.) , whereas an **id** is preceded by hash sign (#).

<style>

.class name {

....CSS code.....

}

</style>

2. An **Id** is unique and it only refers to one HTML element. But a **class** can refer to multiple elements.

The following styling information added to **class** *optionVal* will be applicable to all HTML elements which belong to **class** *optionVal*.

```
.optionVal{
    width:250px;
    height:50px;
    font-family:Comic Sans MS;
    font-size:20px;
}
```

> In this example, the **<select>** and **<option>** tag belong to **class** *optionVal*. So any text written within these two tags will have a *font size* of *20px*, *font type* will be *Comic Sans MS*, the *field width* will be *250px* and *height* will be *50px*.

Run the above piece of code..

> Refresh *dogs.html* or open the *HTML* folder -> right click on the *dogs* HTML file -> click **Open with** -> select and click **Google Chrome** *(or any other browser you like)*.

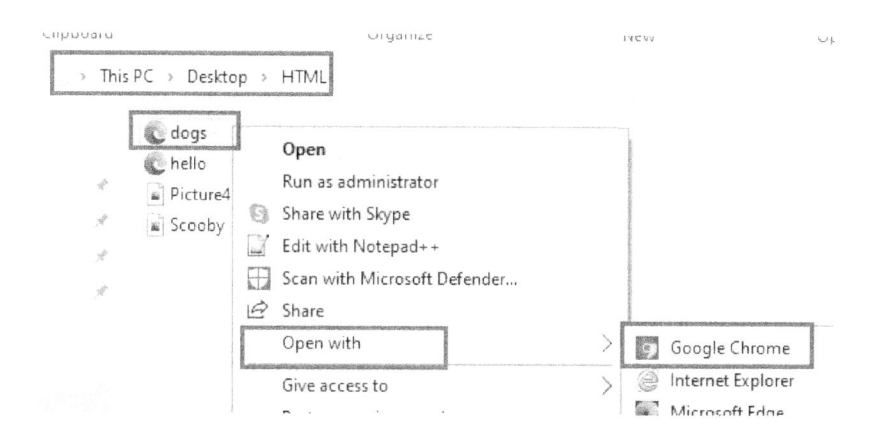

75

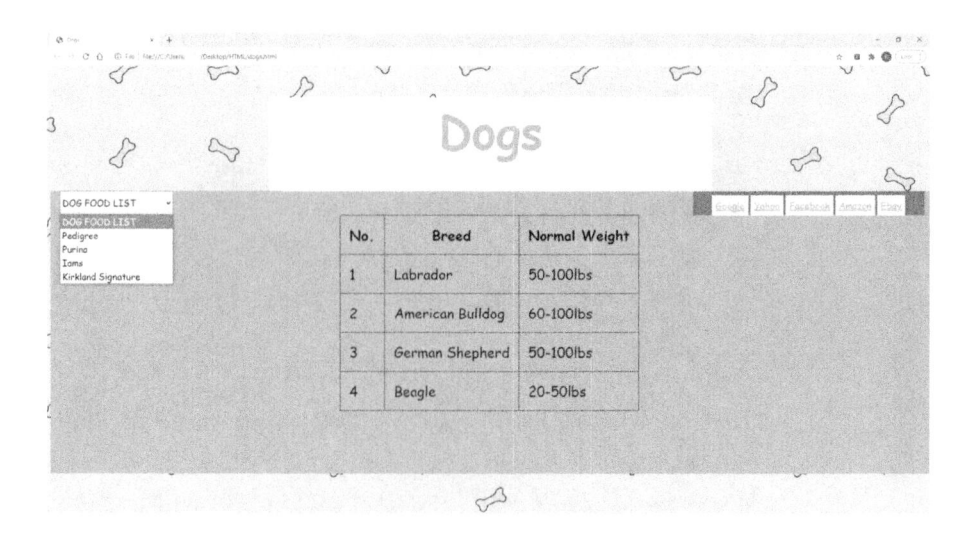

Let's summarize the above process:

1. We already have our parent container (with **ID** *main*) which we created in section 3.1.4.

2. We created our child container and gave an **ID** name *drop_down* *(highlighted in the screen shot below).*

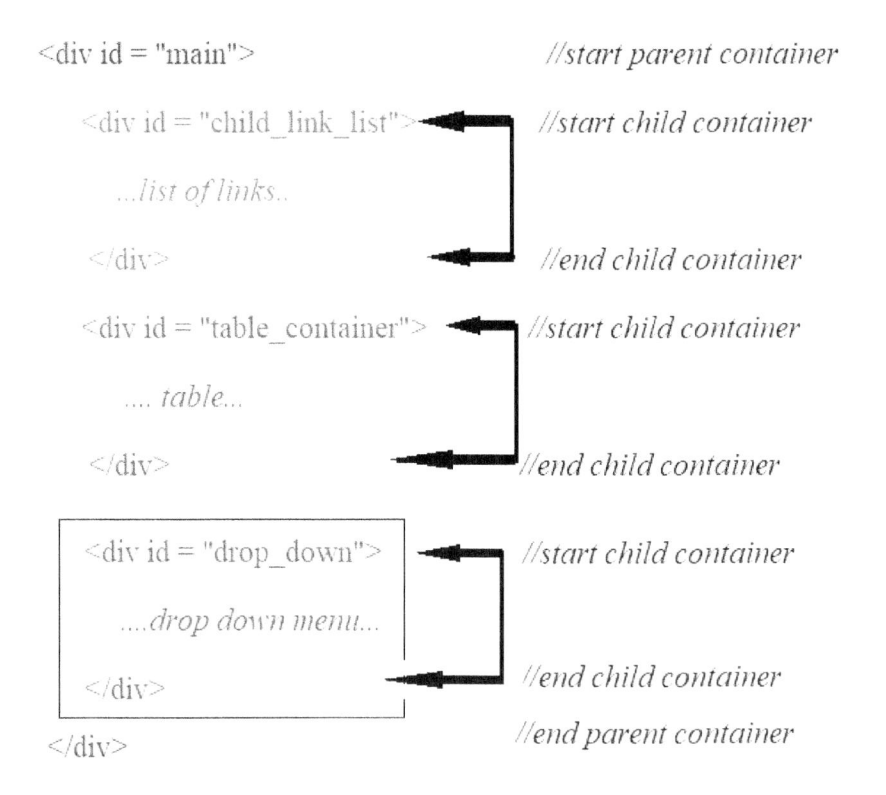

```
<div id = "main">                    //start parent container
    <div id = "child_link_list">     //start child container
        ...list of links..
    </div>                           //end child container
    <div id = "table_container">     //start child container
        .... table...
    </div>                           //end child container
    <div id = "drop_down">           //start child container
        ....drop down menu...
    </div>                           //end child container
</div>                               //end parent container
```

3. We positioned the child container to the top left side of its parent container *(shown in the screen shot below as **child container 3**)* using CSS **position properties**.

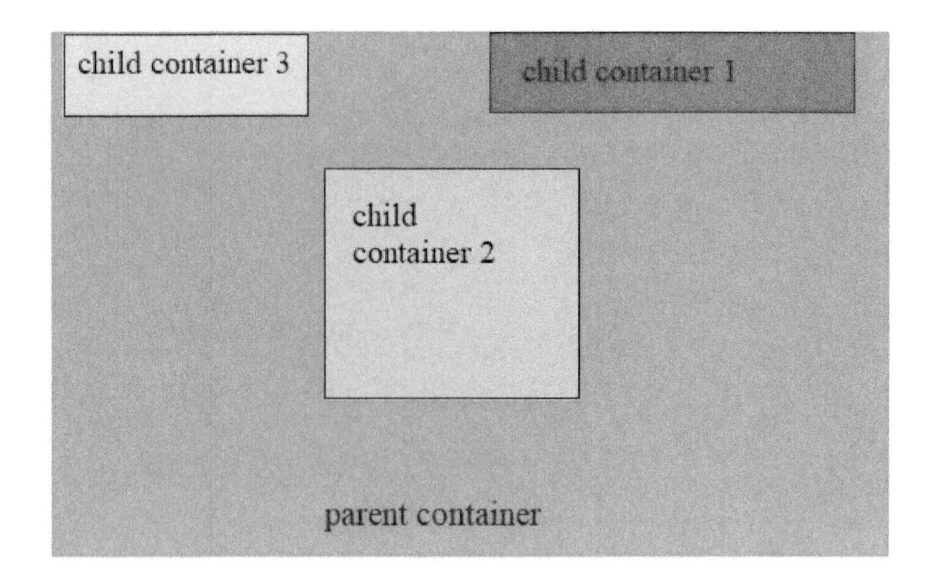

[Diagram: parent container holding child container 1, child container 2, and child container 3]

4. We created the drop down menu within the child container. The **\<select\>** tag and **\<option\>** tag belong to a **class** *optionVal* and its styling information is common to all HTML elements *(\<select\> and \<option\>)* which belong to **class** *optionVal.*

3.1.7 : Add input fields

Let's create another container within the parent container with **ID** *main* (created in section 3.1.4) and this child container will hold all the input fields.

```
</table>

</div>

<div id = "drop_down">

   <select class = "optionVal">
        <option class = "optionVal"
        <option class = "optionVal"
        <option class = "optionVal"
        <option class = "optionVal"
        <option class = "optionVal"
   </select>

</div>
```

```
<div id = "input_section">

</div>
```

I assigned an **ID** name *input_section* to the child container *(highlighted in the screen shot above)* and gave the following styling information to it *(shown in the screen shot below)*:

```
#input_section{
     position:absolute;
     top:100px;
     right:150px;

}
```

position property discussed in section 3.1.4.

This child container will hold all the input fields. So let's create the input fields.

```
<div id = "input_section">

    <input class ="input_fields" type = "text"
    placeholder = "Enter Dog Name">

    <input type = "submit">

</div>
```

To the **<input>** tag of **type text**, I assigned a **class** name *input_fields* (*shown in the screen shot above*) and gave the following styling information to it (*shown in the screen shot below*):

```
.input_fields{
        width: 180px;
        height:30px;
        font-family:Comic Sans MS;
        font-size:20px;
}
```

> ➤ I set the *width* and *height* of the input field using CSS **width** and **height** property. Then I set the *font type* and *font size* of the text used within the input field using CSS **font-family** and **font-size** property.

Run the above piece of code..

> ➤ Refresh ***dogs.html*** or open the ***HTML*** folder -> right click on the ***dogs*** HTML file -> click **Open with** -> select and click **Google Chrome** (*or any other browser you like*).

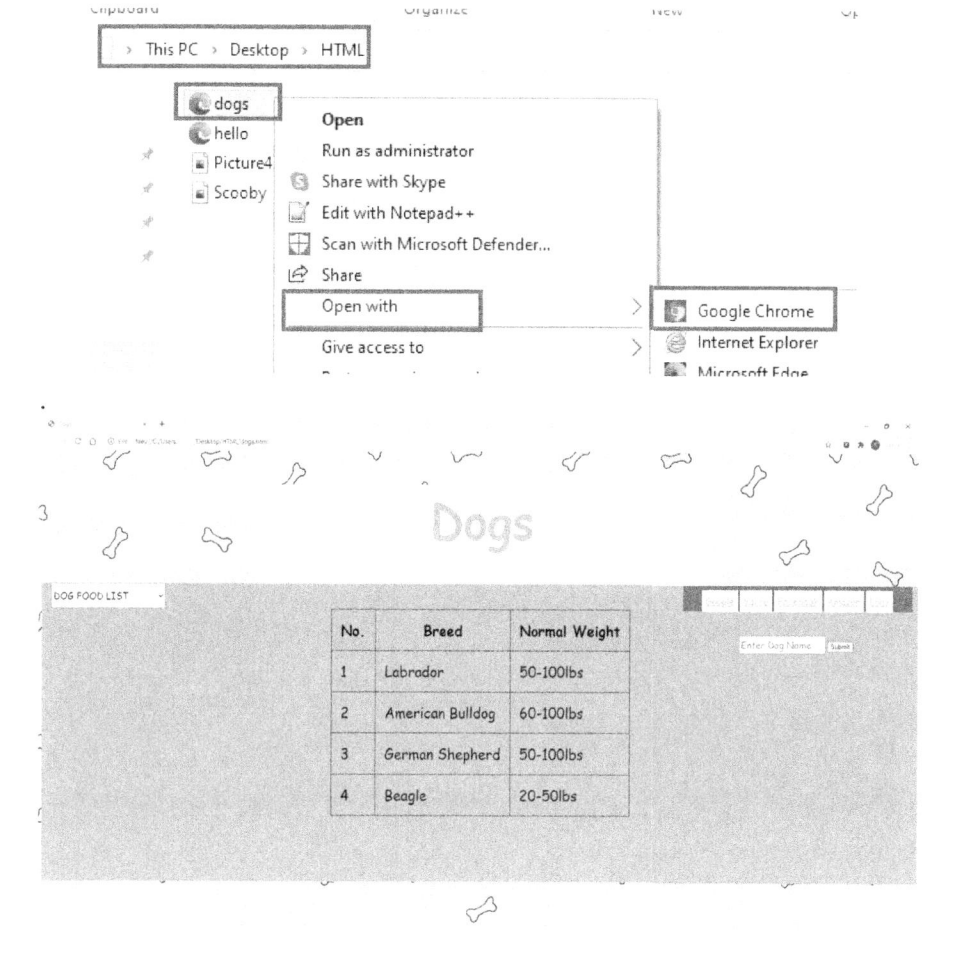

Let's summarize the above process:

1. We already have our parent container (with **ID *main***) which we created in section 3.1.4.

2. We created our child container and gave an **ID** name ***input_section*** *(highlighted in the screen shot below).*

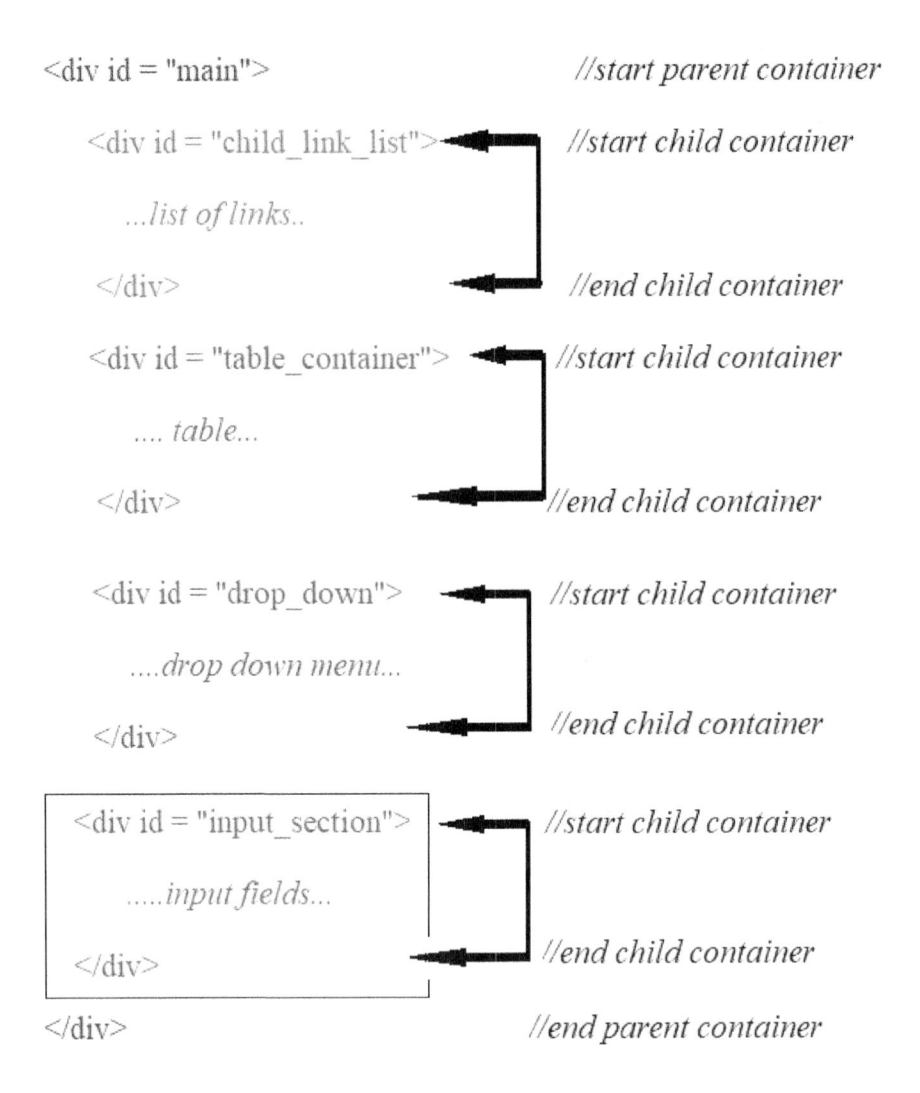

```
<div id = "main">                        //start parent container
    <div id = "child_link_list">         //start child container
        ...list of links..
    </div>                               //end child container
    <div id = "table_container">         //start child container
        .... table...
    </div>                               //end child container
    <div id = "drop_down">               //start child container
        ....drop down menu...
    </div>                               //end child container
    <div id = "input_section">           //start child container
        .....input fields...
    </div>                               //end child container
</div>                                   //end parent container
```

3. We positioned the child container to the top right side of its parent container *(shown in the screen shot below as **child container 4**)*.

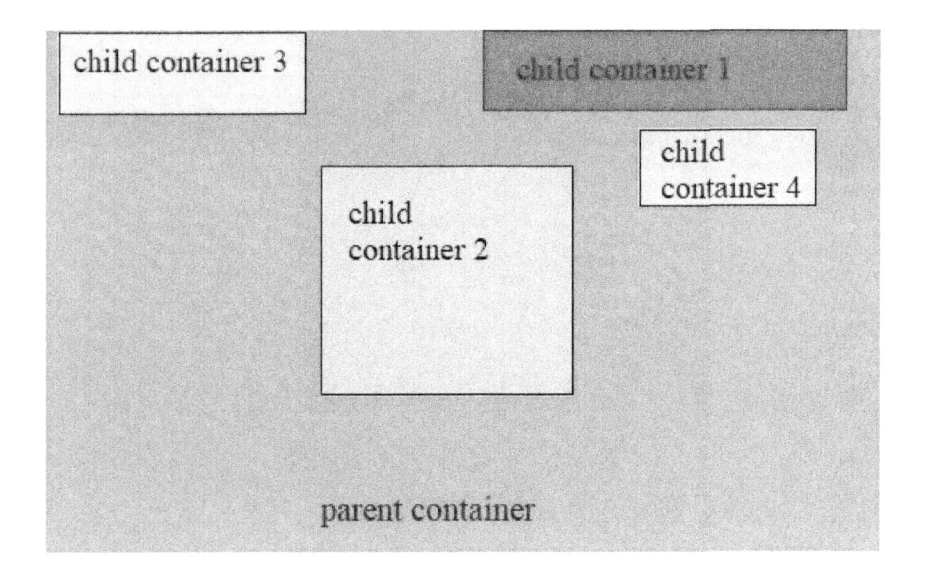

[Diagram showing parent container with child container 1, child container 2, child container 3, and child container 4 inside]

4. The child container holds the input fields.

3.1.8 : Add an image

Let's create another child container *(I gave it an **ID** name **image**)* within the parent container with **ID** ***main*** *(created in section 3.1.4)*.

```
<div id = "image">
</div>
```

The styling information added to this child container is:

83

```
#image{
    position:absolute;
    bottom:0px;
    left:0px;
}
```

position property discussed in section 3.1.4

This child container will hold the image. So let's add the image.
```
<div id = "image">
<img id = "pic" src = "Scooby.jpg" alt = "pic">
</div>
```

Please note: Since *dogs.html* and the picture *Scooby.jpg* are present in the same folder, we do not have to give the full path in the **src attribute**.

The styling information added to the image is:
```
#pic{
    width:80%;
    height:80%;
}
```

Run the above piece of code..

➢ Refresh *dogs.html* or open the **HTML** folder -> right click on the *dogs* HTML file -> click **Open with** -> select and click **Google Chrome** *(or any other browser you like)*.

84

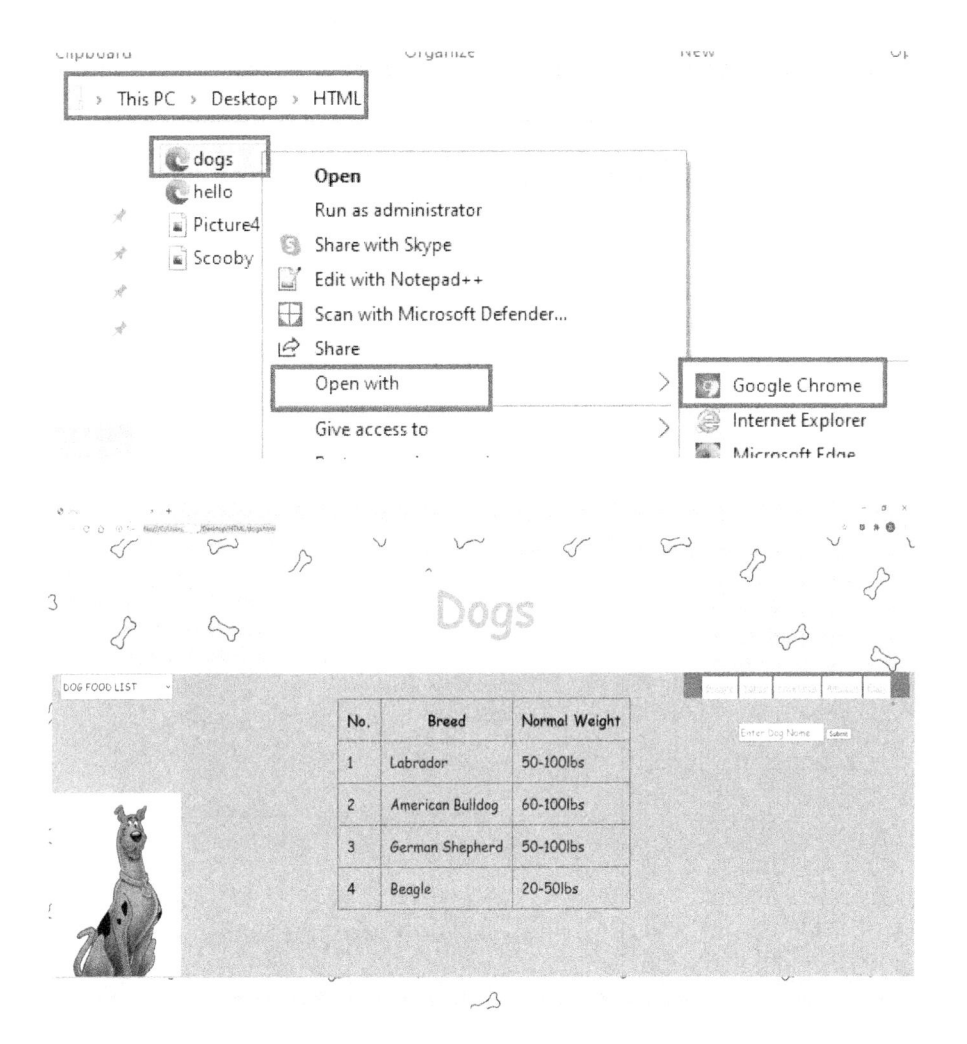

Let's summarize the above process:

1. We already have our parent container (with **ID** *main*) which we created in section 3.1.4.

2. We created our child container and gave an **ID** name *image* *(highlighted in the screen shot below).*

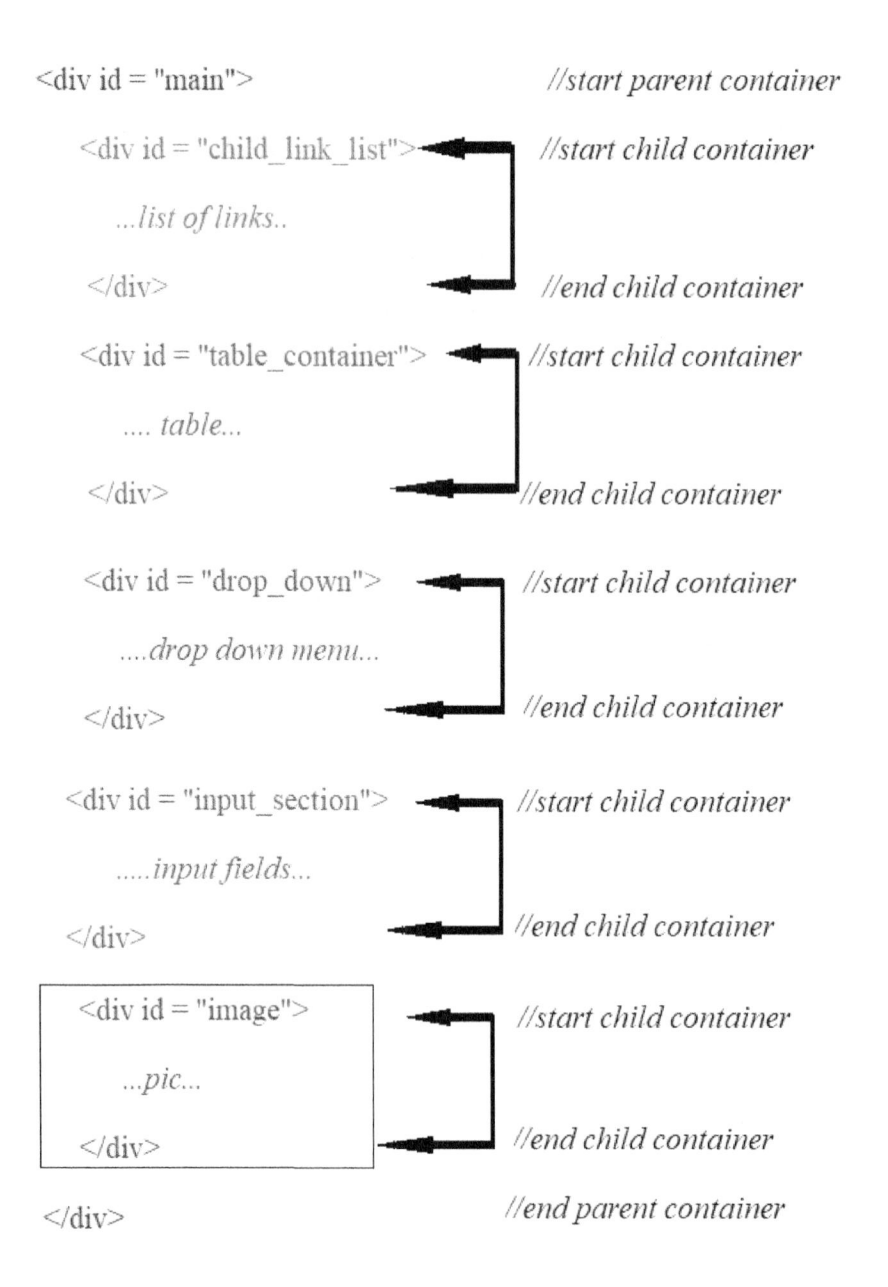

```
<div id = "main">                    //start parent container
    <div id = "child_link_list">     //start child container
        ...list of links..
    </div>                           //end child container
    <div id = "table_container">     //start child container
        .... table...
    </div>                           //end child container
    <div id = "drop_down">           //start child container
        ....drop down menu...
    </div>                           //end child container
    <div id = "input_section">       //start child container
        .....input fields...
    </div>                           //end child container
    <div id = "image">               //start child container
        ...pic...
    </div>                           //end child container
</div>                               //end parent container
```

3. We positioned the child container to the bottom left corner of its parent container *(shown in the screen shot below as **child container 5**)*.

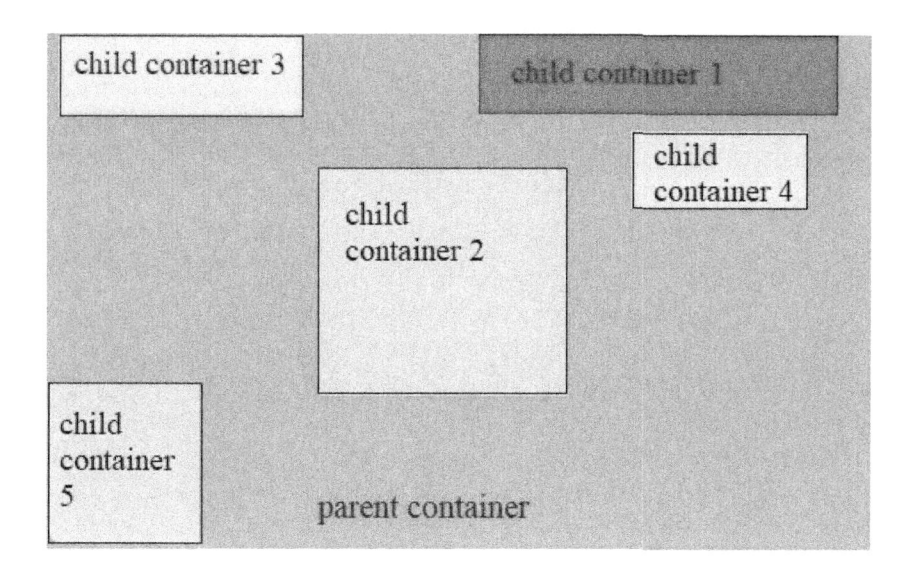

```
child container 3                    child container 1

                                              child
                                              container 4
                        child
                        container 2


    child
    container
    5         parent container
```

4. This container holds the image.

Additional Information:

What is CSS Opacity property?

CSS **opacity** property is used to make an image transparent. Lesser the value more transparent the image will be. The default value is 1.

Syntax:
opacity: *value*
The value can be 0.1 or 0.2 or 0.3 and so on.

3.2 : External CSS

Important points to note in External CSS are:

- In External CSS, we write our CSS code in a separate file and link that file with our HTML document using **<link>** tag.

87

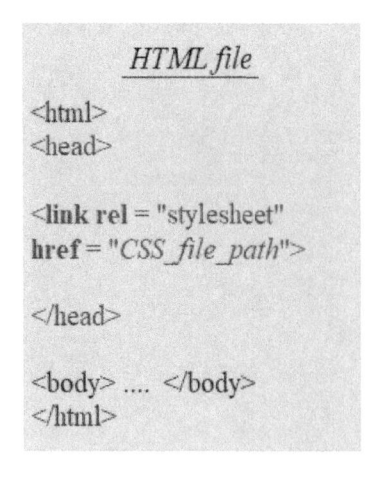

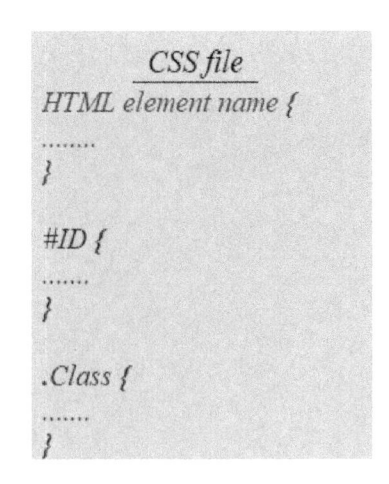

```
        HTML file
<html>
<head>

<link rel = "stylesheet"
href = "CSS_file_path">

</head>

<body> .... </body>
</html>
```

```
         CSS file
HTML element name {
.........
}

#ID {
.......
}

.Class {
........
}
```

rel attribute *provides the relationship between the current document and the linked document. The linked document is a* **stylesheet**

```
<link rel = "stylesheet" href = " ..........................  ">
```

href attribute *provides the path to the stylesheet*

- By separating the CSS code from HTML codes, makes the HTML document look cleaner and less complicated.

Example:

➢ Open **Notepad++** -> create a new file -> give the ***File name*** *(I named my file **externalCSS**)* and ***Save as type*** *Cascade Style Sheets (*.css) and save it in **HTML** folder (created in chapter 2).*

↑ › This PC › Desktop › HTML

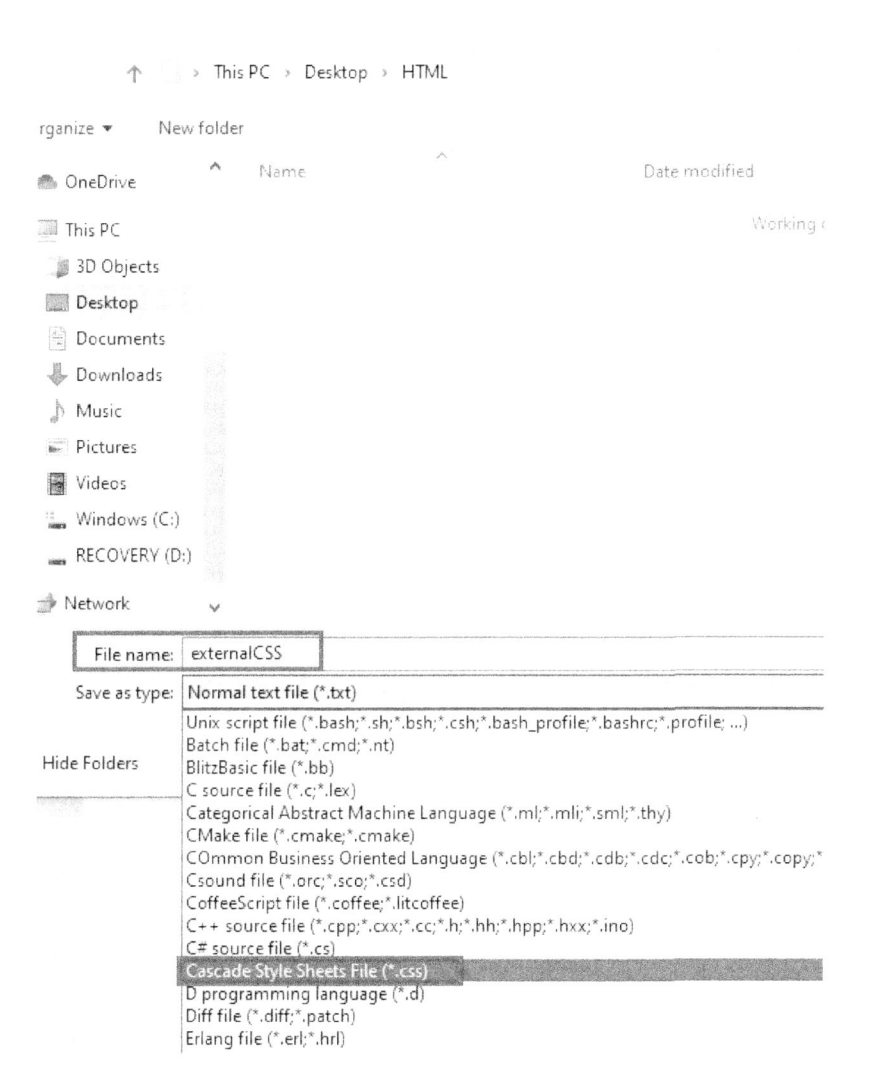

rganize ▼   New folder

- OneDrive
- This PC
  - 3D Objects
  - Desktop
  - Documents
  - Downloads
  - Music
  - Pictures
  - Videos
  - Windows (C:)
  - RECOVERY (D:)
- Network

Name   Date modified

Working

File name: externalCSS

Save as type: Normal text file (*.txt)
Unix script file (*.bash;*.sh;*.bsh;*.csh;*.bash_profile;*.bashrc;*.profile; ...)
Batch file (*.bat;*.cmd;*.nt)
BlitzBasic file (*.bb)
C source file (*.c;*.lex)
Categorical Abstract Machine Language (*.ml;*.mli;*.sml;*.thy)
CMake file (*.cmake;*.cmake)
COmmon Business Oriented Language (*.cbl;*.cbd;*.cdb;*.cdc;*.cob;*.cpy;*.copy;*
Csound file (*.orc;*.sco;*.csd)
CoffeeScript file (*.coffee;*.litcoffee)
C++ source file (*.cpp;*.cxx;*.cc;*.h;*.hh;*.hpp;*.hxx;*.ino)
C# source file (*.cs)
Cascade Style Sheets File (*.css)
D programming language (*.d)
Diff file (*.diff;*.patch)
Erlang file (*.erl;*.hrl)

Hide Folders

89

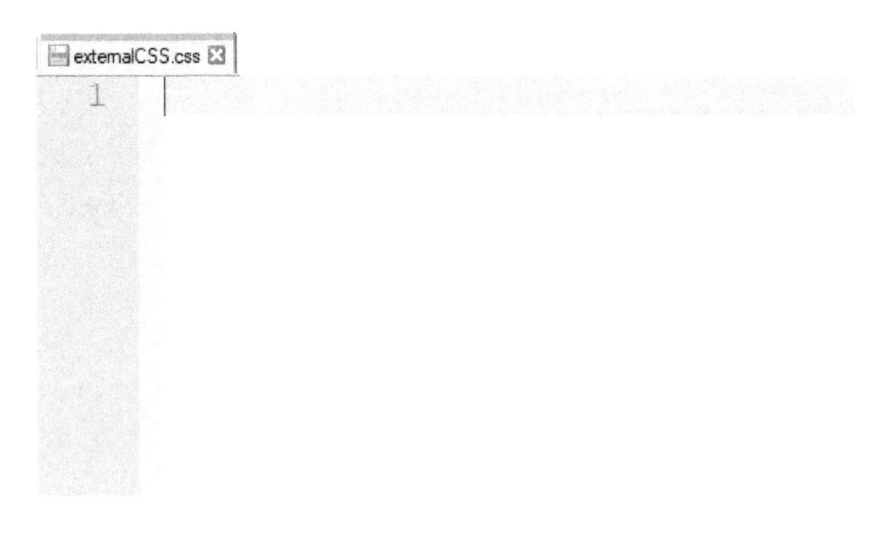

➢ Open *dogs.html* *(created in section 3.1)* file in **Notepad++** and copy all its CSS code written within <style> tag and paste it in *externalCSS.css* file.

```css
body{
    background-image: url("Picture4.jpg");
    background-repeat:repeat;
    width:100%;
    height:100%;
}

#heading{
  width: 50%;
  height: 200px;
  background-color: white;
  margin-left:auto;
  margin-right:auto;
}

h1{
  font-family:Comic Sans MS;
  font-size:100px;
  color: orange;
  text-align:center;
}

#main{
    width: 100%;
    height: 600px;
    background-color: orange;
    position:relative;
}

#child_link_list{
        position:absolute;
        top:0px;
        right:20px;
        background-color: red;
        width:500px;
        height:50px;
}
```

```css
li{
  display:inline;
  text-decoration:none;
}
a{
  padding:8px;
  color:orange;
  font-size:20px;
  font-family:Comic Sans MS;
  background-color:white;
}

a:hover{
background-color:gray;
}

#table_container{
    position:absolute;
    top:50px;
    left:33%;
}

table,td,th{
    border: 1px solid black;
    border-collapse: collapse;
}

td,th{
    padding: 20px;
    font-size:30px;
    font-family:Comic Sans MS;
}

#drop_down{
    position:absolute;
    top:0px;
    left:20px;
}
```

```
.optionVal{
    width:250px;
    height:50px;
    font-family:Comic Sans MS;
    font-size:20px;
}

#input_section{
    position:absolute;
    top:100px;
    right:150px;

}

.input_fields{
    width: 180px;
    height:30px;
    font-family:Comic Sans MS;
    font-size:20px;
}

#image{
    position:absolute;
    bottom:0px;
    left:0px;
}

#pic{
    width:80%;
    height:80%;
}
```

> After successfully transferring and saving all CSS code form *dogs.html* file to *externalCSS.css*, delete the CSS code with <style> tag in *dogs.html* file and replace it with one line of code highlighted in the screen shot below.

93

```
dogs.html
<!DOCTYPE html>
<html>
    <head>
        <title>Dogs</title>

        <link rel = "stylesheet" href = "externalCSS.css">

    </head>

    <body>

      <div id = "heading">
          <h1>Dogs</h1>
      </div>

      <div id = "main">

        <div id = "child_link_list">

        <ul>
            <li><a href = "https://www.google.com/">Google</a
            <li><a href = "https://www.yahoo.com/">Yahoo</a:
            <li><a href = "https://www.facebook.com/">Facebo
            <li><a href = "https://www.amazon.com/">Amazon</
            <li><a href = "https://www.ebay.com/">Ebay</a><
```

Save everything and run the above piece of code.

➢ Refresh *dogs.html* or open the *HTML* folder -> right click on the *dogs* HTML file -> click **Open with** -> select and click **Google Chrome** *(or any other browser you like).*

94

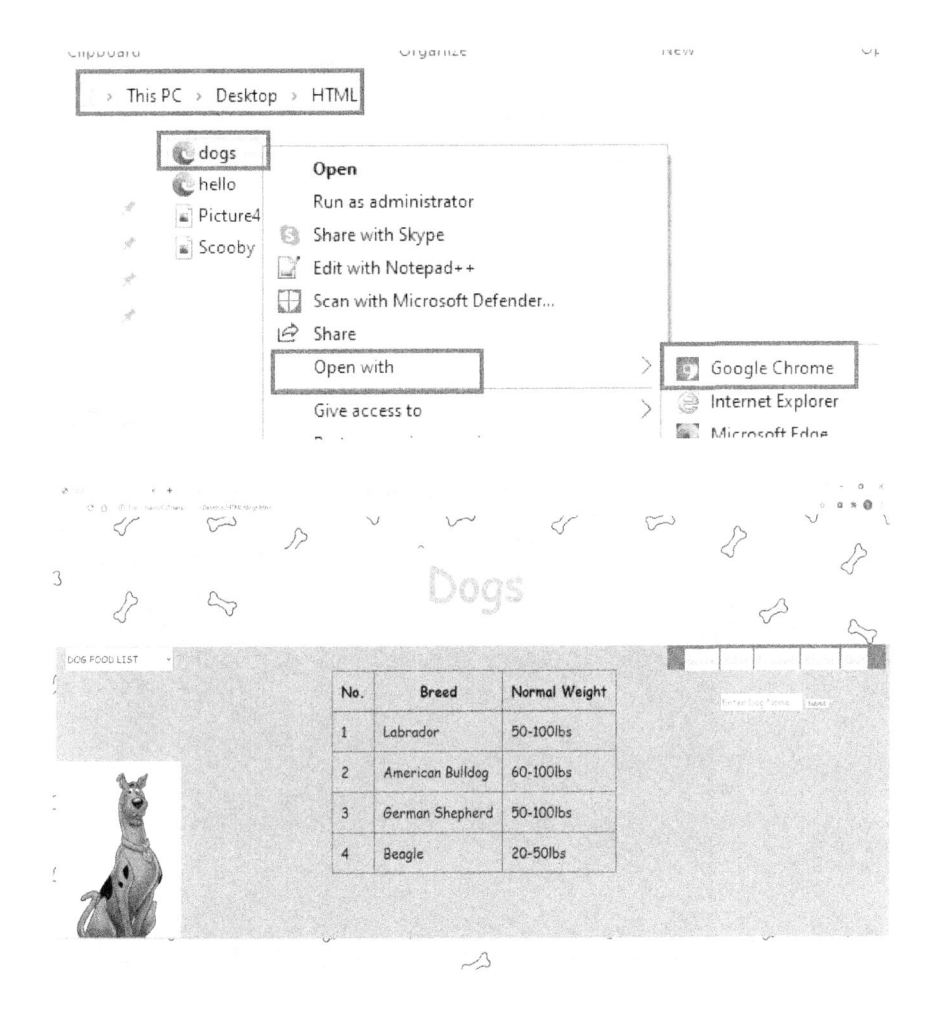

3.3 : In-Line CSS

Few important points to note in In-Line CSS are:

- In In-Line CSS, the styling information is added with the HTML element by using the **style** attribute. Example:

    <h1 style = "font-family : Verdana;"> Hello World </h1>

- Developers usually avoid In-line CSS because:

    1. It makes the HTML code look messy and big. The best practice is to separate the content and the design portion.

    2. As our HTML document starts to become big and complex, In-line CSS becomes confusing and harder to maintain.

    3. It is time consuming.

Chapter 4 : Assessment

Create a website of your choice. The website must contain a Home page with **heading, image, table, links, drop down menu** and an **input field with a submit button**. Once the submit button is clicked, it should be redirected to another page other than Home page (Hint : Use HTML **form**).

Style your pages with CSS and your website must contain **position properties** .

NOTE : You can submit your project folder at test4u.s.basu@gmail.com and I can give you a grade out of **15** (2 points each for heading, image, table, links, drop down menu and an input field with a submit button and 3 points for opening a new page from your Home page).

Wish you all the best and thank you very much for buying this book.

Always remember, the most important learning is Self-Learning..

Printed in Great Britain
by Amazon